LETTERS
TO THE HOUSE CHURCH MOVEMENT

Real Letters. Real People. Real Issues.

RAD ZDERO

Copyright © 2011 by Rad Zdero

Letters to the House Church Movement:
Real Letters. Real People. Real Issues.
by Rad Zdero

Printed in the United States of America

ISBN 9781613790229

All rights reserved solely by the author. The author guarantees all contents are original and do not infringe upon the legal rights of any other person or work. No part of this book may be reproduced in any form without the permission of the author. The views expressed in this book are not necessarily those of the publisher.

Unless otherwise indicated, Bible quotations are taken from The Holy Bible, King James Version (KJV). Copyright © 1977, 1984 by Thomas Nelson Inc., Publishers; The New American Standard Bible translation (NASB). Copyright © 1960, 1962, 1963, 1968, 1971, 1972, 1973, 1975, 1977, 1995 by The Lockman Foundation; and The HOLY BIBLE, NEW INTERNATIONAL VERSION® (NIV). Copyright © 1973, 1978, 1984 by International Bible Society. Used by permission of Zondervan Publishing House.

Quotes from the following were used by permission:
Roger Gehring, *House Church and Mission: The Importance of Household Structures in Early Christianity*, 2004, Hendrickson Publishers, Peabody, Massachusetts. Used by permission. All rights reserved; Charles Trombley, *Who Said Women Can't Teach?*, 1985, Bridge-Logos, Alachua, Florida, Used by permission. All rights reserved.

Library of Congress Cataloging in Publication Data
Main entry under title: *Letters to the House Church Movement*
Zdero, Radovan (Rad), 1969—
1. Christianity.   2. Mission.   3. House Church.

Inquiries about potential non-English translation projects and English editions printed outside the USA and Canada should be directed to the author (Rad Zdero, rzdero@yahoo.ca).

Cover design by XulonPress.com and Rad Zdero
Photo of author by Rad Zdero

www.xulonpress.com

DEDICATION

To my mother Ana Zdero (1942-2010)
who taught me to pray as a child

To all those who went before us in bringing the fires of
renewal, reform, and revival to the church and the planet

To friends and coworkers who are walking alongside
me in this journey called the house church movement

To the one who rescued me, who loves me more than
I often realize, and with whom I will spend an awesome
eternity indeed—Jesus Christ

ACKNOWLEDGEMENTS

All throughout this project, I felt that this was indeed the Lord's idea and that I was merely a junior partner in what he wanted to do. For this privilege, and for the opportunity to interact with so many people in the house church movement from around the world, I am grateful to the Master.

I thank my sister Dr. Jelica Zdero and my friends Dr. Mark-John Bruwer and Ed Peng for reading the manuscript and giving me valuable feedback. Any shortcomings of the book are, of course, of my own making. I appreciate Neil Cole, Joel Comiskey, Tony Dale, David Garrison, Andrew Jones, and Wolfgang Simson for taking the time to consider this book and for writing an endorsement for it. Thanks to the team at Xulon Press for helping get this book published.

The friendship of my sisters and brothers in the emerging world house church movement has been a constant boost and reminder that there are indeed "seven thousand" others (1 Kings 19:14-18).

Thanks also to my friends a little closer to home for being themselves: generous, supportive, fun, faithful, enjoyably eccentric, prayerful, and passionate about Christ.

ENDORSEMENTS

"Letters have always been a powerful means to spread ideas, whether New Testament epistles, presidential correspondences, or fictional letters from Uncle Screwtape to Wormwood, his younger demon apprentice. In this work, we are allowed access to the mind, wit, and passion of Rad Zdero, one of the key leaders in the global house church movement, and there is much to learn. His entries about women in leadership and apostolic leadership alone are well worth the purchase of this valuable resource. This book provides great insights into church but also sets an example for us of how to graciously respond with balance and integrity to people that seem to stand against what God is doing today."

Neil Cole
Foundational Architect of Church Multiplication Associates
Author of Organic Church, Organic Leadership, Church 3.0,
Journeys to Significance, and Search and Rescue
www.CMAresources.org

* * *

"When I want advice about house churches or the house church movement, I go to Rad Zdero. Rad is not only knowledgeable about the house church movement, he also offers clear explanations about what it is and how it works. Rad is also a practitioner, as you'll discover in this hands-on, practical book, Letters to the House Church Movement."

Joel Comiskey, Ph.D.
Founder of Joel Comiskey Group
www.JoelComiskeyGroup.com

* * *

"People say that good things come in small packages, and I would say that Rad's new book, Letters to the House Church Movement, falls into this category. These are real letters into real situations, sensitively, but clearly written over the years. Common sense, a deep concern, and a love for solid, scriptural responses mark this engaging attempt to reach out and deal with a wide variety of issues. This book is great value for any who have a heart and a vision that goes beyond their own church to the church at large."

Dr. Tony Dale
Physician and businessman
International house church coach
www.house2house.com, www.simplechurch.com

* * *

Letters to the House Church Movement

"For more than two decades, Rad Zdero has labored to usher in a new/old paradigm in church life. It is new, because it is forgotten. It is old, because it is first century. In Letters to the House Church Movement, Zdero invites us inside his efforts in a courageous, candid, and vulnerable publication of the letters that have chronicled his journey. This is an important work that will benefit all who seek to understand and learn from Zdero's experience."

David Garrison, Ph.D.
Missionary and author of Church Planting Movements
www.ChurchPlantingMovements.com

* * *

"There are plenty of entry-level books on the why and how of starting house churches but few that deal with deeper and more practical issues. Considering the sheer scale of the recent global house church movement, this vacuum is inexcusable. Which is why I am thrilled that Rad Zdero has released this series of insightful letters into book form. Letters to the House Church Movement is a collection of responses, questions, and solutions that tackle actual house church issues ranging from handling money to relating to traditional churches to dealing with in-house zealots. These are all questions I have had to answer myself and I will no doubt refer to Rad Zdero's book in the future as a timely, biblical, poignant yet gracious response to real-life concerns, written in a manner remarkably similar to the early church correspondence that now forms our Scriptures. Highly recommended!"

Andrew Jones
Founder, Boaz Project
Blogger, www.TallSkinnyKiwi.com

* * *

"A significant part of the New Testament consists of letters, real-life interaction on Kingdom issues written by at least five folks, Paul, Peter, John, Jude, and James. The fairly recent global re-emergence of the age-old Kingdom blueprint of ekklesia—house churches and regional churches—has led to much enthusiasm and excitement, but also to tensions and questions from those yet unfamiliar with this historic phenomenon. Rad is one of those that has taken the time to sit down, addressing diligently and with wisdom many issues and questions that arise with this, and give us all a sort of house church FAQ that unzips and unpacks the current revolution and makes it more tangible than ever. Many have planted, Rad (and others) have watered, may God give the increase!"

Wolfgang Simson
Author of Houses that Change the World
www.StarfishPortal.net

PREFACE

LETTER TO THE READER

Dear Reader,

May this letter, and book, find you doing extremely well in all areas of your life. As you probably know, God is doing something extraordinary in our day. He is reshaping much of the global body of Christ back to a simple, organic, New Testament-style house church movement. The winds of change are blowing through the church. Time would fail to tell all the many stories of how ordinary people are accomplishing extraordinary exploits for God's empire. From the underground house churches in China where Christian leaders are respected based on their time spent in jail to the Basic Christian Communities of Latin America which engage and empower the forgotten and marginalized. From the church planting movements of the Baptists where the faithful gather in homes and storefronts in groups of 10 to 30 people to the spiritual explosion in India which now has an estimated 1 million evangelistic house churches. From the petrol crisis that sparked the emergence of thousands of Cuban house churches to the North American church shift which has changed millions of institutional church dropouts to spiritual revolutionaries impacting their families, neighbourhoods, and workplaces. I have documented many of these phenomena in my previous books *The Global House*

Church Movement (2004) and *Nexus: The World House Church Movement Reader* (2007).

So where does this book fit into all this? It is often said that the pen is mightier than the sword. That may be the case. But, the pen is also sometimes your only recourse. And though I've been involved in simple, organic, house churches and small groups since 1985, I've had the privilege of co-labouring, interacting, and corresponding with many individuals and groups in diverse places from 2001 to 2011. A series of letters has been the result. Some were written to challenge or persuade, whereas others were meant simply to encourage the recipient. Some addressed theological issues, while others dealt with on-the-ground practical problems. Some were private communications that were never expected to see the light of day, while others were open and public letters sent to wider bodies of believers. Some were written to close friends, while others were composed for acquaintances or strangers. The aim of this book, therefore, is to present to you, for the first time, an inside look at some of the inner workings, controversies, struggles, victories, and personalities that are emerging from within today's worldwide house church movement.

A few words should be given about the format of this book. Not a few letters were written by hand and/or put in the post the old fashioned way. Few minor adjustments have been made to clarify content or improve flow. So, what you have is a truly genuine collection of original letters. I did not include letters from people with whom I was corresponding for several reasons, namely, protecting their privacy, avoiding the need to obtain permission to reprint their work, and because communication was sometimes only one-way from me. Letters were chosen to provide enough variety to give you a good understanding of the issues at stake. All dates and almost all names of places and people have been removed to ensure privacy. Due to the nature of letters, the reader should not expect a comprehensive discussion on a specific topic or assume my views have not somewhat changed on a matter since the time of the original dispatch. Letters have been grouped into chapters based on who the recipients were, rather than on what topic was discussed. I, too, am not immune to the allure of making choices based on practicality. In many ways, this is my most personal work to date. As such, what you have here is a real slice-of-life from today's world house church revolution. Real letters. Real people. Real issues.

Finally, dear reader, I write with the hope that this modest book will not just satisfy your curiosity, but that it will give you pause to consider what God is doing in the world today and will propel you to complete the task to which the Spirit of God has called you.

Godspeed,
Rad Zdero

CONTENTS

Preface: Letter to the Reader xi
1. Letters to Inquirers 17
2. Letter to a New House Church 25
3. Letters to Troubled House Churches 37
4. Letter to Women in House Churches 48
5. Letters to a House Church Radical 61
6. Letters to Critics of House Churches 78
7. Letters to Denominations and Ministries 96
8. Letters to Elders of House Churches 112
9. Letter to Apostles of House Churches 128
10. Letters to Networks of House Churches 139
11. Letter to a Nationwide House Church Movement 148
    Subject Index 161
    About the Author 163
    More Books by Rad Zdero 165

1
LETTERS TO INQUIRERS

Letter #1

This letter was sent as an automated response to the numerous inquirers who contacted me through my website. However, I also sent this personally to individuals who contacted me through other means. This is the letter I most frequently sent to people asking initial questions about house churches. Although it is a generic letter, it addresses some of the basic questions that people often ask when deciding whether they should get involved.

Greetings!

We are happy to have received your inquiry into the global house church movement.

Who are we? We are a team called the Starfish Network, which is dedicated to planting New Testament-style house church networks that focus on the basics of community, discipleship, and outreach. Each autonomous house church in a network is like a family with its own flavour, but has some key elements in common. Although we are not a formal organization, we seek relational, intentional, and missional partnerships with others of like mind.

What are we doing? The vision we believe the Lord has given us is to encourage the house church movement across Canada.

We are also involved in planting house church networks internationally. Our mission statement is: "To see the kingdom of God established in our cities, regions, and nation by linking arms as a relational, intentional, and missional network of house churches, that train and deploy all believers in Christ to impact others."

Why house churches? House churches are natural, simple, inexpensive, reproducible, and relational, and have interactive meetings where everyone can participate and use their skills and spiritual gifts to benefit others. This kind of environment strongly fosters discipleship and leadership development. No one falls through the cracks. It is no wonder then that New Testament believers, the early church of the first three centuries, subsequent renewal/reform/revival movements, and the most rapidly growing church planting efforts around the globe today utilize house-sized churches of 10 to 30 people.

What are house churches and how are they different? Traditional churches can be pictured as cathedral churches where the home prayer or Bible study group is merely an optional appendage. These home groups usually involve only people who are members of the mother congregation and are not outreach focused. There are usually a few of these small groups floating around, but they are not the main program offered by the congregation. The main thing is the large group Sunday morning service. This is like a bicycle wheel hub (Sunday morning large group) with the odd spoke (home group) protruding out. It can be described as a church *with* small groups.

Cell-group churches are also not like house churches. Although there is much in common between them, a house church is not even a cell group, which belongs to a pyramid structure with a senior minister at the top. In cell churches, there is an equal emphasis on home cell group meetings and traditional Sunday morning worship services in a building. This can be pictured as a hub with many spokes jutting outward from it. This arrangement can be described as a church *of* small groups.

New Testament-style house churches are different from both traditional congregations and cell-group churches dotting our Western landscape. House churches are an attempt to get back to the basics of apostolic churches. Stated positively, each house church is a fully functioning church in itself, with the freedom to partake of the Lord's Supper as a full-meal, baptize new believers, marry, bury, exercise discipline, and chart its own course. Usually, each house church has between 10 and 30 people involved. Consequently, house churches can be explained using the principle that church *is* small groups. No buildings, one-man leadership, expensive programs, or highly polished services are required. They are typically characterized by the following: open meetings where everyone can participate (1 Cor 14:26; Eph 5:19; Col 3:16; Heb 10:25); meet mainly in homes (Acts 16:14-15,29-34, 20:20; Rom 16:3-5; 1 Cor 16:19; Col 4:15-16; Philem 1:2); networks of house churches (Acts 8:1, 9:31, 20:17-20; 1 Cor 1:2; 2 Cor 1:1; 1 Thess 1:1; 2 Thess 1:1); local house churches led by unpaid leaders (Acts 14:23, 20:17,28-30; 1 Tim 1:5-9; James 5:14, 1 Pet 5:1-3); and traveling apostolic leaders who are financially supported when needed (Luke 10:1-11; 1 Cor 9:1-5)

House church networks? House churches should become part of citywide or regional networks (Acts 20:17,20) for health, stability, growth, leadership training, and mutual accountability, like a spider web of interlocking strands. We, therefore, advocate tightly working house church networks rather than stand alone, isolated, independent groups. The network functions this way: monthly house church leaders/elders meetings, occasional large group events, and circuit riders that flow from house church to house church.

If you would like more information, we would recommend the following resources. Good websites are www.housechurch.ca, which has free articles and training manuals in the "Resources" section, www.house2house.com, which has an excellent free online house church magazine, and www.ntrf.org, which has excellent free articles from the New Testament Restoration Foundation. Good books can be purchased from www.MissionBooks.org and include Rad Zdero (2004), *The Global House Church Movement*, and Rad Zdero (editor) (2007), *Nexus: The World House Church Movement Reader*.

If you would like to chat further informally, would welcome a free seminar on house churches for your church or interested friends, or have a house church going and would like to plug into a regional network of house churches near you, feel free to contact us.

Peace of Christ,
Rad Zdero

Letter #2
The following letter was written to a married couple inquiring about starting a house church with their friends. They once drove a long way to visit with my house church and attend a conference to get some initial ideas. The aim of this letter, originally written by me on behalf of my co-labourer and myself, was to offer them help as they got started.

Hi Friends,

I hope this letter finds you both doing well in all areas of life, such as family, finances, socially, occupationally, and spiritually. I wanted to connect with you as I haven't seen you since the house church conference back in June and hope that you are encouraged in what God is doing in your lives.

As for me, there are a number of things to update you on. I have been given an opportunity to teach at a university for a semester and am excited about that. Although career stability has been a challenge these past two years, the Lord has kindly decided to move the chess pieces around the board in my favour in recent days. I am thankful.

As far as ministry is concerned, I am excited about the fact that our little network now includes four house churches really pulling together in the same direction. The leaders of these groups continue to meet together every month as a team. We are also enjoying the cross-pollination that happens every couple of months as we try to invite everyone from these churches to a celebration, party, and prayer time. We are more convinced of our own need to network in this manner for growth and stability and relish our connections with others in the region like yourselves. Please find enclosed some brochures that we make use of. They may be of some interest to you. Although there is a good-sized car ride between our respective homes, we wonder if there is anything we can do to encourage you in what you are doing or sensing the Lord calling you to do? Is there anything we can pray for? Is there any way we can make ourselves available? Pray for courage and encouragement for us.

Also, for your information, Wolfgang Simson, author of *Houses that Change the World*, is coming to our area for two days to be the keynote speaker at a conference we are helping with. The details are attached. Know that you come to mind now and again and prayers do go up on your behalf.

Love, peace, joy, Jesus,
Rad Zdero

Letter #3
This letter was sent to an inquirer who contacted me through my website. He was involved in a Christian group living communally, sharing their finances, farming the land, and withdrawing from the "world system." He asked how house churches understood and applied the economic order of Acts 2.

Hi Friend,
Thanks for your email. I will take a look at your group's newsletter and your new web page. I agree with you that too often so-called Christianity is informed more by Hollywood than Holy Scripture, and that there has been almost a complete acceptance of the system of this world from an economic, political, and cultural aspect. What we are really talking about here is the difference between "Christendom" and true "Christianity". In my own life, I have made several steps away from the "system" including simple house churches, not voting for political candidates at any

level, being a pacifist, and trying to do my part in preserving the environment.

The other steps you have taken, that of creating a new economic order like Acts 2, is something that I am currently considering. It seems to me, though, that the church in Jerusalem adopted these economic measures, this "Christian communism", as an emergency measure to some degree. Much of the church's experience in Jerusalem post-Pentecost was really, I would argue, transitional (e.g. the Temple, economic communism, 12 local apostles) and it was spread outward. Paul's churches, though, were slightly different, since they had no Temple, no communism, no local apostles, etc.

My question for you is, what do you make of the fact that many Christians in the New Testament era did not live communally or withdraw completely from their jobs and family lives, nor seemed to be encouraged to do so by the apostles, as far as we know? For example, these would include the Ethiopian eunuch, Cornelius the Roman centurion, Erastus the city treasurer, members of Caesar's household who became Christians, etc. It seems to me, our Lord Yeshua did not ask everyone he met to leave their families and follow him, and in fact encouraged some to stay with their families and bear witness to the healing power of Yeshua ha Mashiah. Do you feel they were disobedient to Christ and what it means to be truly Christian?

Even so, the idea of a "household" church in which true community and where sharing resources happens and where there is disengagement from the "world system" on a number of levels, does have an appeal to me. I have experienced this to some degree over the years. I am glad you are sharing these ideas with me. Are you familiar with Jesus People USA, which sounds quite similar to your group? Also, I am currently reading a book by John Seymour called *Bring Me My Bow*. He is the author of the famous book *The Fat of the Land*, in which he explores exactly some of these issues.

Very interesting stuff. All for now,
Rad Zdero

Letter #4

This letter was sent to a gentleman who was unsure whether his family should get involved in house churches. An important issue for them was how the needs of their children could be met adequately, a concern that all parents naturally and understandably have.

Hello Friend,
    You are welcome for my previous reply to your email. Regarding your concern about children, as you can imagine, there are several options, and each house church typically decides on their own situation and how best to address it.
    Parental responsibility is crucial. One thing that is often encouraged is a more Hebrew Old Testament model of raising children in that it should be primarily the responsibility of the parents to bring them up in the Lord, rather than relying on programs or projects run by a church, even a house church.
    Integration is also important to consider. Some house churches attempt to bring the children into every aspect of house church meetings and life as far as possible. There is no special "children's church", but everyone is called to participate and be involved to their level of maturity.
    Special programs can also be included. After worship and communion and dinner, some house churches often do have times where children are taken to a side room to have a time specifically geared for them, while adults and older children get into more serious adult-style accountability and discussion and ministry. But this is seen as supplemental and should never substitute for parental responsibility and the integration approach described above.
    So, there are a variety of options. I hope this addresses the question briefly. Now my question to you would be, what has been your journey that has prompted you and your wife to consider biblical house churches?

All the best,
Rad Zdero

Letter #5

This letter was sent to a gentleman who attended one of the house church conferences I helped organize. He then sent a lengthy email to a number of people stating his questions, concerns, and investigations about how to proceed next. Since he was not part of a house church and was not close to one, he had some friends visiting some nearby house churches to help him decide which group was the best to join.

Hi Brother,

  Good, glad you have someone on the case checking things out. Honestly, patience is needed especially in an intimate church setting, without it things blow up. As for church history, I think that even though things quickly got sucked up by institutionalization, the Lord has always raised up a remnant people in every generation in diverse places who have been more or less faithful to him. The Priscillianists in the 4th century, the Celtic missionary movement of Patrick in the 4th century, the Waldenses in the 12th century, the Anabaptists in the 16th century, the Quakers in the 17th century, the Methodists in the 18th century, the early Pentecostals in the 20th century, as well as the Indian and Chinese house church movements today, etc. The Lord is doing the resurrecting, not us. The real question is, Do you know what the Lord is asking of you personally? Without that answered, it is futile to try to figure things out rationally or just go church hopping. That requires prayer closet time. Stay encouraged.

My two cents,
Rad Zdero

2

LETTER TO A NEW HOUSE CHURCH

✣

A variation of this letter was sent to several new house churches to encourage and warn them as they started on their journey. A request by a member of one of these groups prompted the initial writing of the letter. I then sent letters to a couple of other relatively new groups I knew, since I felt that they could also benefit from its message.

Dear Friends,

I hope this letter finds you doing well. Feel free to read this letter to your new house church or pass it around amongst yourselves, as it may assist your group to bring some hidden issues to the surface. In your communication to me you brought up a very substantial challenge that many house churches are bound to face sooner or later, namely, how to deal with problems and "problem people." I have delayed responding to you because I wanted to give you a more thorough reply, rather than simply giving you some easy steps to implement. I desired to give a more thorough treatment of some scriptural principles, some concepts, and some real-world house church experiences. I hope what I have written below will be of use to your new group as you get started on this journey, in order to better equip you to address future situations that you might also encounter, and also to help you in resolving your current difficulty.

First, let's address the question, what is a house church? A house church is a small group of people that see themselves as a full-fledged church, but which meets in a home or other convenient place like a coffee shop, a board room, a storefront, and so forth. Inquirers and critics sometimes wonder if house churches form to react against the flaws of institutional churches, to avoid pastoral authority, to create a platform for their own ministry, or to rebel against legitimate forms of church life. Based on the house churches I personally know, the surveys I have studied, the books I have read, and the leaders with whom I have interacted from many nations of the world, this is not the case. Certainly, there are and always will be a few folks and groups here and there who have started their house church for all the wrong reasons. But, the vast majority of house church believers want to recapture the spiritual passion, power, principles, and patterns they see in the New Testament. They recount that believers' meetings and evangelistic gatherings in the New Testament often happened in people's homes. The early Jewish Christians in Jerusalem numbered in the thousands, meeting in the temple courts and from house to house (Acts 2:46, 5:42). The apostle Peter preached Christ to Gentile non-believers gathered in the home of Cornelius the Roman officer (Acts 10:1-48). The apostle Paul trained the believers in Ephesus publicly and from house to house (Acts 20:20). Priscilla and Aquila hosted a church in their home (Rom 16:3-5; 1 Cor 16:19). Nympha hosted a church in her house (Col 4:15). Philemon, Apphia, and Archippus cohosted a church at home (Philem 1:2). Needless to say, you are in good company by meeting in homes and other convenient places, rather than in special church buildings. You need not fear the criticisms of outsiders or entertain personal doubts about whether or not your practice of meeting house to house is a legitimate biblical pattern. Let this issue be finally put to rest.

Second, let's ask the question, what do house churches do? The answer is, quite simply, everything that a New Testament-style church can do. House churches sing and dance, pray and prophesy, study and learn, debate and discuss, evangelize and serve, give and send, eat and celebrate, and weep and laugh. They are full expressions of the life of Christ in their midst as they encounter God, do life together, and engage in mission. In particular, we see in the New Testament a great deal of spontaneity and participation on the part of all believers during meetings (1 Cor 14:26; Col 3:16; Heb 10:24-25). Paul writes, "What is the outcome then, brethren? When you assemble, each one has a psalm, has a teaching, has a revelation, has a tongue, has an interpretation. Let all things be done for edification." (1 Cor 14:26, NASB). So, let me encourage you to give all believers a chance to share what they have from the Lord, rather than letting the talkative ones or those with strong communication abilities to always dominate. One suggestion is that for your first several months, each meeting could be dedicated to one or two people just sharing their life story or ensuring that there is at least a time when you "go around the circle" to speak a few words about what the Lord has done in their life. The main purpose of this is that everyone gets used to talking and hearing everyone else talk. This may seem like a silly exercise at first, and a bit contrived, but it is surprising how many sincere believers are uncomfortable with speaking even to a small group. Bashfulness, whether due to personality or phobia or lack of experience, must be overcome to some degree if the priesthood of all believers is to find its way into the life of a house church. Eventually, people's contributions to the meeting will become more natural and spontaneous as everyone gets accustomed to this type of interaction. Another thing to keep in mind is that, in larger house churches of 20 or 30 people, such participatory and interactive meetings can be difficult to accomplish, so they can form small groups of 2 or 3 that get together regularly for interactive prayer, worship, Bible study, and accountability and then come together with everyone as a larger house church.

Third, if possible, encourage people to move into homes or apartments that are close by to one another in the same neighbourhood, village, or town, or maybe move into the same apartment building. Why? A house church is meant to be a spiritual family, a 24-hour-a-day, 7-day-a-week community. This is the crucible that God can use to change us to be more like Christ. The house church movement is not just about a series of meetings—no matter how good they are—that happen in someone's home. If this is all that it is, we have missed the point. A primary ingredient is building spiritually transforming relationships during the ebb and flow of daily life and ministry. Being close by, therefore, will increase the accountability, encouragement, mentoring, and leadership development that can happen in informal and planned ways. We should never underestimate the power of spending time together doing seemingly ordinary things, like walking, eating, shopping, playing, working, and visiting together. It has been said that more is caught than is formally taught. For example, in one house church in which I was involved, almost all of us lived along the same main street in our part of the city. We were easily within a 20 minute walk of each other, with a few of us being just a few houses apart. Not only did this make our weekly meetings easy to attend, but there were many meals shared, television shows watched, prayers lifted up, spiritual topics discussed, and practical help given as we visited face-to-face frequently.

Fourth, allow godly leaders to naturally arise from within your house church, rather than reacting against the idea of leadership because of bad experiences some may have previously had with institutional church leaders. Why? First-century house churches allowed leaders to arise from within the group who had character, competence, and calling (1 Tim 3:1-7). They were appointed by God himself to be shepherds of his flock (Acts 20:17,28; 1 Pet 5:1-4). One of their roles as more mature, and perhaps more confident, believers in a local body of Christians was to help deal with problems stemming from bad behaviour or bad theology (Tit 1:9-11; cf. Matt 18:15-17, Gal 2:11-21). By way of example, as the main leader of a house church I had planted some years back, I had to deal with a case of overt sin in our group. Money started to disappear from a cookie tin that was used to collect funds for ministry purposes. Nobody confessed to the deed, but several of us were fairly certain about the thief's identity. I took this person to a restaurant for a private meal and asked him tactfully if he knew anything about the missing money, while assuring him that I loved him like a brother. He vigorously denied any kind of wrongdoing. Later in the meal, I asked him the same question a second time, which again evoked his denial. But, near the end of the meal when I asked him the same question for a third time, he broke out into tears and confessed to stealing the money because of his financial problems. He was afraid to confess this to us earlier because he didn't want to be rejected by me or the group. In short, this brother was reconciled to God, to our house church, to me as his friend, and to his own conscience over the next few weeks.

Fifth, consider crafting a basic mission statement and/or doctrinal statement together as a house church. Why? This can help you avoid potentially serious misunderstandings and arguments with people who join your group as to what you are all about. This can help new people decide early on whether or not your house church is something they want to get involved in. This can also remind your group from time to time about what God is calling you to do and what you really believe. Regarding mission, many house churches are wandering the wilderness without any kind of direction or purpose. They are not multiplying new disciples, new leaders, or new house churches. A genuine mission statement from the Spirit of God can help get them out of the wilderness and into the "promised land." Being led by the Spirit, does not mean being aimless and fruitless! After all, the Scripture tells us that "where there is no vision, the people perish" (Prov 29:18 KJV). Examples of Scripture-based mission statements are Matt 28:18-20 and Acts 1:8. Regarding doctrine, some house churches can be very vulnerable to infection from bad theology as new untested people join the group and bring in their own peculiar views, which may be heretical. It is best to filter out these ideas early on before they become a problem. Put simply, there is no point in seeing a vast sea of house churches planted around the world that are heretical. Examples of Scripture-based doctrinal statements are 1 Cor 15:3-8 and Philip 2:5-11. By way of illustration, one house church couple I know quite well used to meet for fellowship with another couple over a period of two years, even gathering together for Bible study and prayer with a larger group of friends. After a few deeper conversations about the teachings of Scripture, it became apparent that the other couple denied the historical Christian doctrines of the trinity and the deity of Christ and believed people should only refer to the Lord Jesus using the Aramaic pronunciation "Yeshua." This discovery was quite shocking for my friends. They never suspected that their friends held to such views. Needless to say that, although they remain friendly, any kind of serious partnership in ministry has become impossible. A simple doctrinal statement may have helped avoid two years of wasted interaction.

Sixth, expect to experience the supernatural work of God through individuals and groups to accomplish the Spirit's purposes. This is like the blood and energy that flow through a body to give it life. Without life, a body is just a corpse that eventually rots and stinks. The same thing can and does happen to house churches that have implemented biblical patterns, but have not experienced the supernatural power of God. To be sure, there have been past abuses and unhealthy obsessions in some previous church traditions with signs and wonders. It is wise not to be too pre-occupied with seeking the miraculous for its own sake. But, our fears or inexperience should not prevent us from being open to this genuine aspect of Christian faith that fills the New Testament page after page. From the New Testament, we know that the power of God can show up through dreams, visions, angelic activity, prophecy, words of knowledge, healings, exorcisms, nature miracles, raising the dead, speaking with tongues, baptism in the Holy Spirit, and so on. How and when this comes about is ultimately up to God. Your responsibility, though, is to be open to whatever the Lord may want to do supernaturally, whether or not it upsets some of your previous theological viewpoints or challenges your fears. One network of house churches I participated in began to see tiny glimpses of this reality. We learned from other believers who had more experience in this, as we prayerfully studied the Scriptures, and as we sought to step out more boldly and take risks by acting on the spiritual authority delegated to us by Christ. I could tell you many stories about this.

Seventh, link your house church into an existing network of house churches in your city, region, or nation, rather than remaining an isolated group unto yourselves. Why? The first-century household churches were connected together in citywide and regional networks through apostolic visits (Acts 15:36), apostolic letters (Acts 15:22-29), large group events (Acts 5:12, 20:20), and leadership meetings (Acts 15:2, 20:17). They were able to exchange resources, receive training, implement accountability, and work together to reach non-believers with the gospel (Acts 2:41-47). Unlike isolated groups, interlinked house churches and leaders today, therefore, can step in when problems arise through a visit or a letter or even a more lengthy conflict resolution process. I cannot tell you how many times I have been asked by house churches whether I know of any other groups in their area. People are hungering to know they are not alone and are looking to partner with others of like mind because they know they will not rise to their full stature in Christ if they continue in isolation. One house church I helped adopt into a regional network, for instance, eventually began to struggle because people in the group were inconsistent in their attendance and were also unfairly putting all the responsibility of planning and leading onto the shoulders of one particular couple who had leadership gifts. This became an ongoing dilemma. A meeting was arranged in which I would visit the group to facilitate a troubleshooting process. The sparse attendance at that gathering spoke a clear message—the so-called members of the group were not really committed to each other as a house church. So, I asked the couple to look at things realistically and consider whether it was time to close the group down officially. They agreed it was. Despite the sense of loss and disappointment, the couple also felt free as the burden of artificially propping up that house church was lifted from them. But this kind of help was only possible because they were part of a network of house churches.

    Eighth, the very nature of a house church opens itself up to great joys and sorrows. How so? Because of the small size of the typical house church, which is usually between 5 to 30 people, everything is amplified. The genuine affection, times of fun, accountability, and practical support can be great indeed. And the turmoil of sin can be minimized, but not avoided altogether, because people are more apt to be mutually transparent, encouraged, and answerable to each other in a trusting environment. Besides, it is much more difficult to hide your struggles and pain in such a small group setting. No one easily falls through the cracks. But, as with all things in life, often the greatest strengths of house churches are also their greatest weaknesses. When problems arise in a house church, they become obvious to everyone and will impact the entire group. The survival of the group itself is at risk. For instance, I have known house churches (including ones that I helped personally start) to lose members or completely close down due to all sorts of issues, whether it be some blatant sin, the death of a member, theological differences, unrequited romantic interest, loss of evangelistic vitality, or just plain old personality conflict. My advice, therefore, is that your house church deals with problems in your midst prayerfully, scripturally, compassionately, clearly, and quickly. Don't let problems fester.

Ninth, a problem or problem person may be a cross your group may need to bear for its own benefit that God has specifically allowed or designed, rather than only seeing it as a bad thing to be merely endured or dealt with. Why? It may be a training tool to instruct your group to learn the art of compassion, persistence, forgiveness, and conflict resolution. It may also be a wake-up call to the reality of community life which brings your group out of the superficial, idealistic, honeymoon phase that characterizes many house churches at their start. It may even be a spotlight that reveals areas of strength and weakness about your group's level of commitment, depth of character, and quality of understanding about what it means to be the church. As an example, one house church that I started a number of years ago was comprised of people who were each, in their own way, completely opposite to me in temperament, education, age, ethnic background, biblical understanding, emotional maturity, and so forth. And, let me tell you, it was sometimes quite frustrating for me to try to lead and develop this house church to become what I believed God wanted it to be. As I look back, I now see how much I learned about my own strengths and weaknesses as a leader, how to deal with other people's flaws, how to promote mutual relationships among a varied group of people who had few things in common, and how

3

LETTERS TO TROUBLED HOUSE CHURCHES

Letter #1

The following letter was sent to a troubled house church I planted by myself and with which I was involved day-in and day-out. It was my own spiritual family and almost always met in my home. Yet, there were some weaknesses that needed to be addressed if it was going to survive and thrive and become all that it was meant to be. Although by no means an ultimatum, I felt it was important to draw a line in the sand to see who really wanted to move forward together as a company of the committed.

Dear Friends,

  I hope everyone is having a really good day today. This letter is about our house church. It's been several months since we met together and I do miss those times as a group, although a number of us have been in touch during this time as individuals. I believe the time is now for this letter. Perhaps it's a little strange to get a letter from me, when we can easily go for a coffee or just pick up the phone. But, I want us to have something in our hands that we can go back to and ponder over and over as we process some ideas individually.

Over the past several months, I believe God has spoken to me personally about my life. So, recently I have been spending concentrated time praying over a number of issues, activities, and responsibilities I had before. I've been taking stock of my life and of our house church. Should I cut out, cut down, or add things to my life? This is where I am at in the process.

As I look back over the past year and a half as a house church, there have been many very good things that have happened, and I have been excited to be part of the group. If we are to continue as a group, though, I believe there are some things that we need to focus on. If you feel the same way and are willing to step up to the plate, then let me know, and we can carry on as a house church. If not, that really is okay, but please let's be honest with ourselves and recognize that maybe we should close down our group. As I see it, there are five things we need to implement if we want to continue as a house church.

We need to be seeking the Lord as individuals. The best way our little church will grow and thrive and be healthy is if we spend time alone with God. He is our greatest source of energy and life and wisdom and protection. This doesn't mean only saying a routine little bed time prayer and once in a while reading a couple of sentences from the Bible. I mean setting aside time each day as individuals dedicated to seeking God with our hearts and minds. If we are able to do this consistently, then I think we have a real shot at being a really spiritually strong group. Will we spend time with God?

We need to be seeking the Lord as a group. When we meet, everyone can and should have something to contribute. God can use us (and has used us) powerfully to speak to each other as the church during our group time, whether it's a brief word of encouragement, sharing an experience of what God has been saying recently in our lives, being honest about a struggle, reading something from our diary, giving a teaching, or speaking up during the meeting if God is saying something to you right then and there. We can have something very meaningful to contribute (a) if we have been spending quality time with God during the week individually, (b) if we are able to cut out distractions that sometimes happen during group time, like too much small talk, joking around, or going off on tangents, and (c) if we are willing to seek God seriously in prayer as a group and even sometimes wait quietly until someone is prompted to speak by the Spirit. Will we invite God into our meetings?

We need to create community among ourselves. A house church, of course, is more than having good meetings. It's also about having meaningful relationships outside our group time. It's about a loving community that cares for one another practically. If we are truly part of one another's lives outside the weekly meetings, then we really will be following Jesus' command to love one another. And some of this good stuff has started to happen in our midst. However, I believe it is possible for us to be even better friends than we have been in the past. I have appreciated everyone's friendship personally, especially over the last couple of months. Thank you all. Of course, our group is very diverse and we have people with very different backgrounds and ages and careers and preferences and family obligations and work schedules, and so on. It can be a challenge for our mixed group, at times, for strong relationships to develop between two very different people. What can that look like? It means both quantity and quality time. It means going out for coffee, chatting on the phone, popping in for a visit, helping mow the lawn, going to a movie, visiting a sick friend together, praying with one another, and so forth. Will we become a tight group that loves one another?

We need to reach beyond ourselves. One of the reasons I came to this city was to start a house church that would outlive me and continue on when I leave. I know God sent me here because he had confirmed it in several unusual ways to me when I was initially seeking him in prayer. Now, a number of good things have been done in and through our house church, such as passing out thousands of evangelistic flyers, getting an introductory outreach Bible study group going during the summer months, developing friendships with neighbours and sharing faith with them, being open to new people joining, giving out a Christmas food basket to a needy neighbour, etc. How people have responded was up to them. Whether new people ever came to our house church for a short season or over a long time was up to them and God. Each of us has a unique personality and we will reach out to people in different ways. And a house church has different seasons—sometimes we should rest and sometimes we should actively reach out to new people. Whatever the case, I believe outreach must be an active and ongoing part of our house church, whether we do so individually or as a group, whether few or many new folks come. The real question is if we are willing to be passionate about the world the way God is.

We need to carefully consider how we build the church. The apostle Paul once wrote that it was important to keep checking the blueprint if you get involved in a building project. He knew that the foundations he was laying when he started churches should be made of strong spiritual material. Otherwise, when trouble comes, the church would be destroyed (1 Cor 3:10-15). In the same way, we should ask how we are building our house church. What should be kept? What should be thrown out? What should be added? What should be adjusted?

Finally, over the next number of days, let's all seriously ask God whether or not he wants us to continue as a house church. And let's seriously ask ourselves if we are willing to consider and implement the particular items above. If you have a strong sense from God about anything—any ideas, any concerns, any questions, or any conclusions—please let me know as I would love to hear about it. If I am the only one left in the end committed to moving forward, do not worry about me. My commitment to the Lord and the New Testament way of living out the gospel will still be intact, for the Lord is my shield and my strong tower.

Thanks my friends. I hope to hear from you soon,
Rad Zdero

Letter #2

The following letter was sent to a troubled house church that was experiencing internal difficulties. There were marriage troubles, a big argument, and people quitting. Although I did not start this group, we developed a close relationship over several years, and I had helped integrate them into our regional network. I was aware of some of the dynamics involved in the group. But, more importantly, I sensed that I personally needed to write this letter to address what was happening, despite my own hesitation.

Hello Friends,

I hope you are all doing well in body and soul. I'm writing because I would like to ask some questions of you to ponder as a house church. Truthfully, I'm hesitant to write anything at all because of how letters like this might be perceived as sticking one's nose where it doesn't belong. But, be that as it may, there are some ideas I want to communicate that you can pray about and consider as a group, especially with all the transitions and turbulence you are experiencing. I hope this note is received in the spirit with which it's written, that of genuine affection for you.

Let me make some remarks about true fellowship. A few days back at our monthly house church network meeting of leaders, we were praying for your house church specifically. I found myself staring at the back of the room for some reason. A painting caught my eye. It depicted Jesus washing the feet of his disciples. This I felt was something from the Lord for your group. You all know the story in John 13:12-15. After washing their feet, Jesus remarks: "If I then, the Lord and the Teacher, washed your feet, you also ought to wash one another's feet. For I gave you an example that you also should do as I did to you." (John 13:14-15 NASB). Yes, you are having some difficulties. Yes, you have a variety of personalities and temperaments in the group. Yes, you all have different spiritual gifts and abilities. Yes, there are even sometimes differences of opinion on what your mission as a group should be. But, all that being said, are you willing to wash one another's feet, as the Lord has washed yours? And what will that mean for you practically as you deal with the challenges you face?

Permit me now to turn to the issue of prophecy in your house church. A few days ago I had a dream. Now, I cannot say 100% for sure that this was a God-given dream or whether it was me just processing things. In the dream, I said these words to some specific individuals in your group: "It is a mistake to think that a prophetic word is supposed to take pastoral effect." As I've pondered this dream, I have some thoughts as to what it means. A prophet's job is very specific—to "speak" what they sense the Lord is saying. Once they have done that, they have done their job. Difficulties sometimes come, however, when the prophet tries to step beyond their job of just "speaking" and tries to "practically implement" the word into reality. The job of weighing the word and practical implementation of the "when" and the "how", rather, must be done by the entire house church as a team (see Acts 16:9-10; 1 Cor 14:29; 1 John 4:1). This may mean that nothing is done with the prophetic word right away in that meeting or in that moment, so that it might sit under the scrutiny of prayer and Scripture and reflection for some time. In addition, we must take care that the very act of giving prophetic words in meetings does not become a substitute for pastorally caring for and teaching one another. Therefore, I ask you, are there things that you can do to make the prophetic process healthier in your house church?

Allow me to comment on the three basic elements of any healthy house church. From my own experience in house churches, it seems that there is a need for a balanced mix of ingredients to be present for a house church or house church network to accomplish what God wants. Any healthy church is like a three-legged stool. This can be expressed by the equation, Truth + Relationships + Mission = Church. The early church had all three aspects in place, not in a programmed mechanical way, but in an organic way as they followed and were empowered by the Spirit (Acts 2:41-47). If one of those legs is missing, look out, you're in trouble! Problems will arise if all three legs are not there. For example, Truth + Relationships but without Mission = a religious social club that can become ingrown. Similarly, Truth + Mission but without Relationships = a religious corporation bent on recruiting members and selling its product. And, finally, Relationships + Mission but with a distorted form of Truth = a cult-like group. Now, there may be times when the Lord will lead you to focus on one particular thing because you may need to learn some lessons. But, this is usually only for a season. And spiritual seasons come and go just like natural seasons. For instance, the Lord may ask you not to do any overt evangelism for a few months because he wants you to focus on prayer. But, if your group then began to claim that the Lord has told you not to share your faith with non-believers for the next 5 or 10 years, then I would become concerned. I would question whether you really heard from God, because he is a missionary God, seeking and saving the lost. Therefore, my encouragement is that you faithfully implement all three essential aspects of what it means to be the church of Christ, unless you know clearly that the Lord is leading you to focus mainly on one of these three aspects for a season. So, I ask you, how is your house church going to make sure that Truth, Relationships, and Mission are in proper balance and are each present in sufficient quantity and quality?

In case you did not know, a decentralized, but cohesive, network of house churches is emerging across your region. So far, this involves about 20 house churches. I encourage you to plug your group into this network. One of the things this will do is to create an opportunity for those whose spiritual gifts are not meant to be used in only one house church, but rather across an entire network of house churches. This is where apostolic, prophetic, evangelistic, and teaching gifts can be fully expressed by those called by God to travel as "circuit riders" from house-to-house and place-to-place (see Acts 2:41-47, 15:36, 20:20, and Eph 4:11-12). Some people, however, may be called to particularly focus only on their own house church as active local believers and/or local leaders. Both are needed. Both are important. We need the ground troops (who focus on the local skirmishes) and the air force (who can see the larger scope of the land) to work together to fight the good fight. Now, I ask you, how are each of you individually processing your own calling in this regard? And, will you actually take the opportunities that God presents to you when they arise in the house churches, whether he wants you to focus locally or whether he wants you to participate across the emerging network of house churches?

Let's consider the idea of "calling." I used to get frustrated and discouraged when things in the house churches did not go the way I thought they should go. I felt like my head was going to pop off and my heart was going to fall out of my chest! And many times I just wanted to quit because it didn't seem like it was worth the effort. But, then something changed, in part due to several of you being faithful in using your prophetic gifts to speak God's word to me. It was almost like a fresh revelation of something I had known in my head, but which had not totally sunk deep into my heart. I came to realize that God was personally inviting or "calling" me, specifically to help spawn the house church movement. The difference this has made is enormous. It has been so freeing. What used to bring me heartache and headache, now barely affects me. Whether this or that thing goes wrong (or right) in the house churches is ultimately not my responsibility. I cannot control outcomes. My responsibility is to pray, study, watch, and obey. When I got my heart around my personal "calling" from God, the supposed challenges and obstacles and difficulties and trials and tensions no longer discouraged me nearly the way they used to. And so, let me ask you, why are you specifically involved in the emerging house church movement? Is it because it's convenient, or meets some personal preference, or seems strategic, or because your friends go, or because you like small groups, or because you like to participate in meetings? These are all valid reasons but, I believe, the main reason always needs to be that you feel personally called into this by the Lord. This makes all the difference in the world. Otherwise, when difficulties come—and they will—you will just leave your house church and go somewhere else and bring a suitcase full of unresolved issues into the new situation.

    Finally, thanks for reading this letter. I hope it's been encouraging, but also challenging. If you think it might be useful for me to visit with you soon to specifically facilitate dialogue, prayer, and Scripture study on these matters further, then I am happy to do so. Besides, I really do love just being with you when I visit anyway!

Peace of Christ,
Rad Zdero

Letter #3

The following letter was sent to a house church populated by a number of younger folks. I appreciated their enthusiasm, and knew and liked them personally. But, there were some concerns I had which I felt I needed to gently address in a letter to the three people who were, in effect, the leaders of the group.

Hi Friends,

Here's hoping this little scribble finds you all doing really well in all areas of your lives, socially, financially, emotionally, physically, family-wise, and spiritually, although I suppose all of life, if one thinks about it, is spiritual in nature. I woke up this morning and had the crazy idea of writing to you. How useful or encouraging or timely this letter is, you be the judge. Whether God asked me to write something or it came out of my own head, I do not know. In either case, I don't write to you as having any authority, other than that which Christ gives to every one of us. I write only as a friend in Christ. Specifically, I write to the three of you—the power trio—as those whom God has tapped on the shoulder to protect and serve the disciples that are with you. That's your job and privilege. But, I do also write to your entire house church, and you have my go ahead to read this letter to them, if you so choose.

Why do you exist as a house church? It seems like a simple question, with a simple answer. Please don't get what I'm saying wrong. I know of a more "regular" church in town here that literally gathers thousands together because of the amazing teaching pastor they have. I know this guy personally. Good guy. But it seems to me that there is so much emphasis on him, that there is a danger of it becoming a little personality cult. They are even going so far as planting some satellite churches in other cities and beaming in his sermons and speeches by video and satellite to the service on Sunday. What happens when and if this guy leaves or some tragedy strikes? I know of another church in which the pastor is a little bit like a rock star to the younger folks. When he's not slated to speak, you can hear the grumbling in the pews. What is this all about? These are all good-hearted pastors and nice people. Perhaps the idolization so common in our society is creeping into the church in some ways. But this should not be the case with you and me. When our house churches gather, may they do so not around a superstar leader, a pet theology, a style of music, or a great hi-tech event. May we gather around Christ, and Christ alone, as we meet as his body. I have said on a number of occasions that all we have to offer as house churches is relationships and Christ. If someone is mainly looking for fancy programs and hi-tech services, they've come to the wrong place. The apostle Paul wrote, "Let the word of Christ richly dwell within you, with all wisdom, teaching and admonishing one another with psalms and hymns and spiritual songs, singing with thanksgiving in your hearts to God." (Col 3:16 NASB).

What happens when you get together? Another simple question, with maybe a simple answer. Again, don't get me wrong. I truly believe that God is working in more "traditional" settings. However, for the most part, Jesus Christ is relegated to being the guest of honour in most churches. People sing to him, people talk about him, and people tell those who haven't heard that they should come and do the same thing. And it is usually a few people at the front performing a service, ceremony, ritual, or show for the many passive spectators sitting in the pews. Remember those days? And, what's more, it is usually—and in some cases exclusively—the paid professional with the seminary degree on the wall, that is allowed to teach from the front. The rest of the people are not using their gifts and abilities given by God. But, Christ does not want to be just the guest of honour when the church gathers. Rather, he wants to be the Master of Ceremonies, directing each of us to contribute and give something to the spiritual "potluck" or "smorgasbord" dinner, so that everyone can benefit. We are to be the body of Christ to one another, loving, giving, teaching, encouraging, and challenging one another. This does not mean, of course, that everyone always has the exact same contribution or the same "air time" (no!), but rather each gives something to the group during the actual meetings based on the spiritual gift they have. Each one has been gifted in a unique way. Yes, that's right folks. Each of us is of value and has the right and responsibility of using our own particular ability when we meet. Let's be ready, willing, and able on those occasions during our meetings when God taps us on the shoulder spontaneously and in the moment to ask us to speak or act. No more spectator Christianity! The apostle Paul asked, "What is the outcome then, brethren? When you assemble, each one has a psalm, has a teaching, has a revelation, has a tongue, has an interpretation. Let all things be done for edification." (1 Cor 14:26, NASB).

Who's the "boss" of your house church? Is it one of the three of you? It certainly isn't me. The true head of the body of Christ is Christ himself. He's the man with the plan. Sure, every church says that. All Christians agree. All house churches say the same thing: "We have no King but Jesus!" But are we really letting the Spirit lead us? Do we even recognize the Spirit's voice? Jesus said that his sheep hear his voice. But, do we? If not, we are playing church again. Yes, the three of you do have a God-given responsibility to be the spiritual guard dogs of your house church. As such, you have to listen to Christ too (I mean really listen). Otherwise, it's to the doghouse for your house church. And mine too!

Okay, I'll stop for now. Enough said. Let me just end off by saying sorry if this letter seems a bit out of place or inappropriate time-wise or otherwise. I write simply to encourage you and remind you of some things, not as anyone having authority over anyone else. I write as a friend. I am just as accountable to you, as you are to me. And if there is something you wish to write or share with my house church or me, please do so. May the *true* force be with you!

Peace out! With affection,
Rad Zdero

4

LETTER TO WOMEN IN HOUSE CHURCHES

This letter was sent to several friends I had known well and with whom I worked closely in the cause of the Christ. They felt free as women to use their skills and resources in their own house churches and among the wider body of Christ. I wanted to encourage them to keep doing so and to provide some scriptural and practical foundations on the issue. Expecting they would meet other women who were unsure of their proper role in the family, society, and church, I hoped this letter would equip them to be encouragers in those cases.

Dear Sister,

    Here's hoping this letter finds you doing exceptionally well in all things. This is a personal note to you and a few other sisters in Christ whom I know well and who have been my coworkers in the gospel. I write because I want to encourage you to find your freedom in Christ as a woman and to be all that you are meant to be. I write because I know that many sisters feel like second-class citizens of God's empire and, for some reason, have yet to find their place in it. I am certainly not a "feminist" who wants to liberate women and cut the chains of male oppression for the sake of an ideology or cause. But I am certainly not a "chauvinist" either who wants to minimize and marginalize women in the church because of some inherited traditions of male domination. Rather, I consider myself a "biblicist" who wants the Bible to deeply and authoritatively inform my own opinions and practices. Although I have written an article on the topic which has been read in some circles, I'd like to expand on the theme. Although by no means do I claim to have it all figured out, I'd like to briefly share my own understanding of what the New Testament actually says about a woman's role in the church and then move on to some practical applications for the simple, organic, New Testament-style house church movement that God is raising up today. I trust this letter is received in good faith. I welcome your response.

What are the common views on women in today's church?

The Ultra-conservative view says that women should never have any authority over, or even teach, a man. The Male Leadership view believes that women can teach but never have formal leadership in the church. The Pluralist Leadership view says that spirit-led leadership is open to both men and women, since formal "ordination" as practiced in many denominations is not really biblical anyway. The Egalitarian view suggests that the same ministries and formal leadership roles are fully open to both men and women. The Ultra-liberal view says that it's about time women take the reins of leadership away from men in society and in the church, since it is their human right to do so. Each of these views, and those in-between, are motivated by different things. Ultra-conservatives look to the past in their effort to preserve so-called traditional family values, where the father is the decision-maker and breadwinner and where the mother is the stay-at-home subservient caretaker of hearth and home. The good thing about this is the increased sense of security and stability that comes to a society and church in which people know where they fit. Taken to an extreme, however, this approach forever imprisons women into a fixed role of bygone days without any room for flexibility or creativity or personal calling. Ultra-liberals, on the other hand, look to the future as they promote a so-called democratic human-istic agenda which fights for the equality of the sexes where men and women have the same opportunities, responsibilities, and rewards. The good thing about this is the increased sense of personal freedom in society and in the church to pursue one's calling and destiny and dreams with all the passion one can muster. Taken to an extreme, however, this approach artificially erases any distinction between men and women and in its place creates one monstrous androgynous being that, in its own way, is now imprisoned by the social expectation to be all and do all. And sandwiched in-between sit the various combinations of these understandings. For the most part, sincere Christians will make an appeal to the Bible for support. Yet, ironically, this issue will continue to be debated and will not likely be resolved until the Lord Jesus finally returns. I, too, am no different in this regard and wish to first lay out my own understanding of the matter from a biblical standpoint.

What does the New Testament say?

Women were apostles. In Rom 16:7, Paul greets two outstanding apostles. One is a man named Andronicus. The other person's name, however, could either be read "Junias" (male) or "Junia" (female), depending on where the accents are placed. The problem is that Greek copies of the New Testament in the first 700 years did not place accents on names. Even so, other evidence overwhelmingly favours the female name "Junia." Why? First, there are over 250 inscriptions and references in ancient Greek and Latin literature in the city of Rome alone to the common female name "Junia." Second, there is virtually universal agreement up to about 1300 AD by church leaders and theologians that the female name "Junia" is meant. Third, no evidence whatsoever exists from the Greek and Latin literature of the day that the male name "Junias" ever even existed. Fourth, no evidence whatsoever exists that the known male name "Junianus" was ever shortened to "Junias" or any other form. Finally, no good evidence exists linguistically or historically that Rom 16:7 should be translated "well known *to* the apostles." For the definitive work on the topic by an eminent New Testament scholar, see Eldon Jay Epp's book, *Junia: The First Woman Apostle*.

Women were prophetesses. Anna was a prophetess (Luke 2:36-38), and Philip's daughters prophesied (Acts 21:8-9). Peter said that women could prophesy (Acts 2:17-18). Although she was criticized for heresy and immorality, Jezebel was not rebuked for calling herself a "prophetess" (Greek = *prophetis*) (Rev 2:20).

Women were evangelists. A woman spread the good news about Jesus and saw many in her town come to faith (John 4:39-42). And Jesus chose Mary Magdalene to be the first witness and herald of his resurrection (John 20:15-18), despite the fact that a woman's legal testimony was worthless in that society.

Women were teachers. Priscilla and her husband privately corrected Apollos on doctrine (Acts 18:26). Although rebuked for heresy, Jezebel was not rebuked because she "taught" (Greek = *didaskein*) (Rev 2:20).

Women were elders. Some scholars suggest that women were included in the list of qualifications for overseers/bishops (i.e. elders, pastors) and deacons by the gender neutral word "man" (Greek = *tis*, meaning "someone") (1 Tim 3:1) and the connecting word "likewise" (Greek = *hosautos*) (1 Tim 3:11). This does not mean Paul is mechanically applying the list he gave for male overseers to women overseers, since this would mean that women should also be the husband of one wife. That would make no sense. Rather, I suggest, Paul's main point is that overseers, whether male or female, must have their personal and family lives in order.

Women were deacons. Phoebe in Rom 16:1-2 is called a "deacon" (Greek = *diakonos*), meaning "servant." She is also called a "minister" (Greek = *prostatis*), meaning one who "presides" or "sponsors." A form of *prostatis* is also used regarding overseers/elders (1 Tim 3:4-5, 5:17).

Women were Paul's coworkers. Euodia, Mary, Persis, Phoebe, Priscilla, Syntyche, Tryphaena, and Tryphosa are either referred to as "coworkers" by Paul or described as having "worked hard" for the gospel (Rom 16:1,2,3,6,12; Philip 4:2-3). Surely, this involved teaching and preaching.

Women were heads of their households. Mary, Lydia, and Chloe were the leaders of their household (Acts 12:12, 16:14-

15,40; 1 Cor 1:11). A "household" (Greek = *oikos*) was really a circle of influence that included family members, servants, friends, and business associates who used the house as a social and economic centre. And Priscilla's name appears before her husband Aquila's on four of six occasions, which in that culture meant that she was more prominent than her husband (Acts 18:2,18,26; Rom 16:3; 1 Cor 16:19; 2 Tim 4:19).

Women were hosts of house churches. Mary, Lydia, Nympha, and Priscilla hosted churches in their homes, a highly prominent role in that culture (Acts 12:12, 16:14-15,40; Rom 16:3-5; 1 Cor 16:19; Col 4:15). And Apphia hosted and likely co-led a house church with Philemon and Archippus (Philem 1:1-2).

Women were full participants in church life and mission. They could pray, prophesy, teach, encourage, and use all their spiritual gifts (1 Cor 12:7-12,27-28, 14:26; Col 3:16; Heb 10:24-25). And during Jesus' ministry, women materially supported his work and hosted him at home (Matt 27:55-56; Luke 10:38).

What about 1 Cor 14:34-35?

Let me suggest that Paul is not giving his own view here, but he is actually *quoting* his *opponent's* slogan or saying by which they sought to silence women in the church. Why? First, there is *no* Old Testament scripture or "law" that specifically silences women, so it could not be Paul who was making this appeal to keep women quiet. Second, however, there were dozens of Jewish man-made "oral laws" of the *Talmud* that did seek to silence women, which Jewish legalists would naturally have appealed to. Third, the language style used here is not typical of Paul. Fourth, the passage disrupts the natural flow of the previous discussion on spiritual gifts and totally contradicts the idea of everyone's participation, which Paul just finished writing about in 1 Cor 12 and 1 Cor 14. Fifth, this passage is followed by an "expletive of disassociation" indicating disapproval (Greek = $\bar{e}$, pronounced "ay" and meaning "what?!", "nonsense!", or "no way!").

So, what is happening here? Basically, Paul just finished writing at length in 1 Cor 12 and 1 Cor 14 that *everyone* can participate in church life and church meetings using their spiritual gifts. Then in 1 Cor 14:34-35, Paul *quotes back* to the Judaizers (i.e. the legalists) their own man-made "law", which would silence women completely. Then in 1 Cor 14:36-40, Paul responds to the Judaizers with passionate disapproval of their man-made "law" and that they should heed his previous instructions to allow for prophecy and full participation by everyone, including the women. For a detailed discussion see Charles Trombley, *Who Said Women Can't Teach?* chapters 1-4.

What about 1 Tim 2:11-12?

Almost all New Testament letters were written in order to deal with a local problem. This passage, therefore, can easily be understood as a situational, temporary, and appropriate silencing of women because of their participation in an early Christian heresy (i.e. Gnosticism) in the Ephesian church, rather than a universal or general silencing of women in the church. Consider the following two problems Paul was confronting in Ephesus that should shed light on the passage.

First, Paul prophesied earlier about heresy that would enter the church in Ephesus (Acts 20:29-30). False teachers eventually did begin to promote fables and particularly influenced some gullible women, who became disruptive with these ideas (1 Tim 1:3-7, 4:1-7, 5:11-15, 6:3-5, 20-21; 2 Tim 3:6-7, 4:1-4). In fact, 1 Timothy addresses many early Gnostic heresies (Greek = *gnosis*, meaning "knowledge")(1 Tim 6:20-21). What was Paul to do? His solution was that, until the situation changed, Paul tells these women to keep quiet temporarily (Greek = *ouk epitrepo*, meaning "I am not permitting", rather than "I never permit.") (1 Tim 2:11-12).

Second, early Gnostic teachers explicitly taught that Eve was superior to Adam, that Eve was created before Adam, and that she opened the way to true godly "knowledge" by eating the forbidden fruit in Genesis. See the early Gnostic texts *The Hypostasis of the Archons* and *On the Origin of the World*. What was Paul to do? Paul reminded them, however, that Adam was created before Eve, and that Eve was actually deceived by her pursuit of such special "knowledge" (1 Tim 2:13-14). For a detailed discussion see Charles Trombley, *Who Said Women Can't Teach?* chapter 16.

Paul was not appealing to the book of Genesis to prove that men should be leaders over women or that men are superior, but rather he wanted to show the Gnostics that they had the wrong ideas about the true origins of creation, humankind, and sin.

Practical applications for women in house churches?

First, sister, identify your spiritual gifts, preferences, resources, and skills so you can understand how God has designed you and what you may be called to do as a woman. Of course, this is not always an easy task, since God sometimes takes his time to unveil his plans for us through the Scriptures, the Spirit's inner promptings, circumstances, and wise counsel. But, it is amazing how many Christians I have met who are unsure of their gifts or calling. This may be understandable for young believers who are just starting to walk with the Lord, but what is the reason for this once people have been believers for many years? This uncertainty may be especially true for women who have grown up in ultra-conservative backgrounds and who have been told all their lives that their main duty before God is to get married, have kids, and follow their husbands. Some women may feel no real sense of individualized giftedness or destiny to which to aspire, but rather a fixed role and responsibility that one simply steps into. There are many good resources out there, such as personality-type tests and biblically-based spiritual gift questionnaires to help you understand yourself. Also, ask others who know you well for their input. I once did a self-test questionnaire, for example, and then asked a few close Christian friends in my house church network to fill it out to assess their perception of me. It was good to know that the strengths and weaknesses I thought I had generally agreed with theirs; I wasn't totally off the mark. Yet, some of the most significant input in recent years has come from prophetic words given to me by house church friends and virtual strangers at house church events. All of these gave me "permission" from the body of Christ to launch out in the direction I strongly sensed from God, like a race horse jumping full-speed ahead when the starting gate was lifted.

5

LETTERS TO A HOUSE CHURCH RADICAL

Letter #1

This letter, along with Letter #2, #3, and #4, was sent to the elder of a house church with whom I was developing a friendship over a period of about a year and a half. We were getting to know each other, we had met together, and he had visited my house church to explore the possibility of working together. But, there were a number of substantial philosophical and practical differences that prevented us from partnering together.

Hi Brother,
 Thanks for the email. I was going to write a more specific one, but wanted to at least let you know that I had read yours and will make some general comments.
 First, allow me to make some general non-Scripture based comments. You have done a very good job at trying to put together the pieces of the puzzle, and I congratulate you on doing so, because most people don't even bother to get into the detail of Scripture. I wish more Christians would move along from milk to meat the way you do. This is a good exercise to sharpen each

other, and I welcome the opportunity to do so, as many Christians will not try to engage on the level of depth or detail as we are now. Although this is a good thing for us to do, it is important to keep in mind that many things are continually in-house debates, so to speak, and that many issues which have divided believers in the past are secondary (e.g. ecclesiology, pneumatology). I consider primary issues the identity and deity of Christ, the nature of the resurrection, the nature of the triune Godhead, the nature of salvation, etc. We are known primarily as disciples of Christ by our love for one another, not in having every detail of theology figured out to 100% certainty.

Second, it is important in my view to not just read the Bible in trying to understand the Bible. If we do, then we are in danger of misunderstanding the intent of the writers and how the readers received the message. I take it as a fundamental principle that it is extremely important to understand the context in which the occasion of the writing occurred, e.g. language, culture, mindset, local situation, metaphor. We cannot assume that our 21st-century mindset is able to accurately and faithfully grasp the meaning of Scripture fully without knowing the foreign context or soil because, whether we know it or not, we bring our own set of suppositions to the table when reading the Bible or anything else. We must clear that away as much as possible in order to understand the Bible. In addition, experience, reason, and tradition are important tools that we bring with us to the task.

Third, regarding the Mystery Babylon issue, you start by asking, "Is there a professing Christian religious system in our world today that is contrary to the New Testament church?" The problem here is that this is a leading question, in which you are starting out with the answer and conclusion you say you wish to look for. One cannot assume, from the start, that a false religious system that is portrayed in the Bible in symbolic terms, is necessarily going to be a professing "Christian system." Similarly, there are important steps that are missed in the essay, which need to be asked before proceeding in the argument and coming to the conclusion that all institutional Christian churches are Mystery Babylon. These questions need to be addressed first satisfactorily before any attempt at identifying more traditional Christian churches with Mystery Babylon. This is a serious charge as you are aware. You need to answer these questions also to really prove your point. Does the Bible in fact talk about a false religious system at all? If so, was it a specific system that existed only at the time of the particular biblical writing? Or, did it survive after the closing of the New Testament canon, and is it around today? Is Mystery Babylon a religious system or some other kind of system, i.e. political, economic, a nation? If it is around today, is it clearly identified by a particular religious organization or is it more of a corrupt mentality and outlook shared by many professing religious people from all sorts of different religions and cultures (i.e. Muslim, nominal Christian, Hindu, etc) that persecuted true Christian believers? If Mystery Babylon is "Christian" on the outside in nature, then is it to be equated with some corrupt parts of the Christian church (i.e. liberal and nominal Christians, Mormons, Jehovah's Witnesses, the medieval Roman Catholic Church) or with all traditional looking Christian churches, even the ones with basically sound biblical theology? What are the other options as to its identity?

Fourth, you say that Mystery Babylon is false Christianity because of its buildings, its steeples, its brick, and its mother city (Rome). Now, allow me to suggest some other possibilities, based on the same logic and Scriptures, that Mystery Babylon may be, in fact, other things. What are some of the main elements that Scripture tells us about Mystery Babylon from the book of Revelation and Babylon from the book of Genesis? There are four criteria: (1) it persecutes true believers (Rev 17:6, 18:24); (2) it has great economic power (Rev 18:11-19); (3) it has great political and global power and influence (Rev 17:18; 18:3, 9); and (4) it is associated with a tower (Genesis 11:4) and a seven-hilled city (Gen 11:4; Rev 17:9, 18). Who could this harlot, this Mystery Babylon, be? Who fits these main criteria? You suggest that it is the institutional church: Catholic, Protestant, Independent, or otherwise. That is possible. However, it could also be the United States of America, since it meets criteria 1, 2, 3, and 4, the last of which is the World Trade Center towers over which everyone wept. It could be just the Roman Catholic Church of the medieval ages, since it meets all the criteria; today's Roman Catholic Church does not persecute other Christians physically. It could be Communist systems found in places like China and Russia, since they meet criteria 1, 2, and 3. It could be Islam, since it meets criteria 1, 2, 3, and 4, the last of which is Mecca. It could be the Revived Roman Empire in the form of the European Community which is emerging in the days ahead, since it meets criteria 2, 3, and 4, and potentially criterion 1. Mystery Babylon could be a type of any world religious, political, military, or political system that appears throughout history that meet these criteria, with the "seven hills" really being the seven continents that make up the globe. Also, Protestant and Independent churches do not have world influence, politically or economically, and certainly are not physically persecuting other Christians. This is why I don't quite buy into the idea that any Christian church that happens to meet in a building is Mystery Babylon.

Fifth, regarding "bricks for churches", you apply the Scriptures "let us make brick" (Gen 11:3 KJV) and "let us build us a city and a tower whose top may reach unto heaven" (Gen 11:4 KJV) to indicate that the false Christian systems "use brick to make their large edifices" and "the word steeple means a tower...connecting them to Babylon." And you seem to take this literally to argue the point. Then, using the same logic, any churches that have buildings that do not have a steeple and that are not made with bricks (maybe wood or steel and glass) and that meet in a gym or movie theatre, are not part of Mystery Babylon. The force of this argument is not a good one and the weaknesses are obvious.

Sixth, you point out that there are "some believers" in these Christian systems or traditional churches. I would say that there are very many millions and millions of real believers in the traditional Christian church. Almost nobody in North America or Western Europe who has made a serious commitment to Jesus as Lord and Saviour today has done so through the house church movement or biblical Christianity, as you put it. I am a case in point. I was taught as a child to pray and believe in God by my Eastern Orthodox parents. When I was 16 my sister brought home a Gideon Bible, printed, financed, and distributed by people who are part of the traditional church and missions agencies. It was after reading this Bible that I made a commitment to Christ. It was Christian TV that helped me understand the basics of faith and discipleship, because I was not even allowed to go to church at that point by my parents. Lots of tension was there. And it was para-church groups like Campus Crusade for Christ and The Navigators that really discipled me during university and with whom I developed spiritually and grew in my knowledge of Scripture. A great influence on me in developing my inner life has been Henri Nouwen, a Catholic priest and author. The home church movement was not there at all in this.

Seventh, in fact, there are many great men and women of God who have been part of the traditional church, such as Billy Graham, Mother Teresa, Francis of Assisi, William Booth who started the Salvation Army, John Wesley who was a committed Anglican priest till his dying day, D.L. Moody, William Carey the father of modern missions, Bill Pierce who founded World Vision and Samaritans Purse, George Whitefield the Great Awakening evangelist, Charles Finney, etc. Even Watchman Nee, who really got the house church movement going in China, became a Christian through traditional missionaries like Hudson Taylor, who was connected with traditional churches. So, to imply there are merely "some" believers who may be saved, but who are dominated by a clergy or system and have no opportunity to grow and follow Jesus and who are not making a difference for Christ using their gifts, is something, I suggest, not quite in line with the facts of history. As Jesus said, "For no one who does a miracle in my name can in the next moment say anything bad about me, for whoever is not against us is for us. Truly I tell you, anyone who gives you a cup of water in my name because you belong to the Messiah will certainly not lose their reward." (Mark 9:39-41 NIV). So, did God compromise by using Mystery Babylon in these cases, and yet tell people to "come out of her" at the same time?

Eighth, let's turn to the issue of "taking on a name". Paul's words in 1 Cor 1:12-13 and 1 Cor 3:3 are said to be a warning to the church against taking on names, like "of Paul", "of Apollos", "of Peter", "of Christ". I think the whole thrust of Paul's message here is being missed. He is not talking about taking on names, as if that were a bad thing in and of itself, but on the whole issue of division and arguing and separating from each other over disagreements. Taking on names is only a result of already existing divisions, not the cause for it. Paul warns against divisions, not against names. If he was merely talking about names, then why does he include "of Christ" in his warning (1 Cor 1:12)? To follow the argument in the essay to its logical conclusion, Paul is suggesting that we are not allowed even to call ourselves "Christians" or "of Christ" because that would create a division. Surely, this cannot be the case. The fact is that believers are called many names in Scripture by other believers: "disciples" (Acts 6:1 and many other times), "the church" (Acts 5:11, 8:1, 8:3 and many other places), "the faith" (Acts 6:7), "the Way" (Acts 9:2; 19:9, 23; 24:14, 22), and other names by non-believers like "Nazarenes" (Acts 24:5) and "Christians" (Acts 11:26). There is, thus, nothing wrong with names or labels, but it is actual divisions between believers that Paul is concerned about.

Ninth, regarding denominations today, the contemporary scene is that many, if not most, Christians that I know do not care at all about the particular church one is involved in. Very few people I have met have ever identified themselves as Pentecostal or Baptist but rather as Christians who happen to be involved in such-and-such a church. There is so much cooperation between churches and missions organizations today that, I dare say, there is very little serious division at all. Some examples include: The Commission into Russia in the 1990s, which brought together hundreds of denominations and churches and missions groups that worked together to bring the message into Russia; The Alpha Course, the successful introduction to Christianity video course used across denominations and by house churches, which has seen several million participate worldwide with over 250,000 people coming to Christ as a result; Billy Graham, who has partnered with and fostered partnership between many churches of all denominations to see people make commitments to Jesus; and World Vision, which has brought together many denominations to alleviate suffering in many parts of the world. Very few really care about denominational labels anymore, so the argument that there is so much division and confusion is a misleading one. God is doing this I believe for the sake of the coming harvest.

Tenth, let's now talk about "crying against the system." I have absolutely no disagreement with you that many times we need to confront corrupt systems, including religious ones, as the prophets and apostles did, with tough love. I have done it myself a number of times. I do not agree, for the reasons described above, that traditional churches and cell churches or any churches that simply have buildings and clergy are necessarily Mystery Babylon. Some of them may have problems, like the seven Revelation churches, but they are not Mystery Babylon. Some churches may be part of it, like very liberal and nominal groups or those heavily involved in politics and war. I do believe, though, God is dealing today with the global Church, including home churches, in the way he does in the seven letters to the seven churches in Revelation. True, Christ warns, spews, and corrects. But, he also commends and encourages. As such, a prophet's role is not just to correct as you point out, and practice, but also to point out as Jesus did to the Revelation churches, the many good things there are with them (Rev 2 and 3).

Thanks for the chance to respond. All for now,
Rad Zdero

Letter #2
This letter was a continuation of the communication from Letter #1. I felt that some of the ideological issues he kept pressing were beginning to distract me from the work of church planting, evangelism, and discipleship that I felt God wanted me to prioritize.

Hello Brother,

I hope all is well with your walk with the Lord, your family, your work, your ministry, and your rest time. I have read through both your emails and am now responding after a busy time these past two weeks. Thanks for being candid about your views on all matters, the effort you put into composing the letter, and the obvious sincerity underlying it all. I do truly appreciate that. I will try to be as clear as possible in responding to your points.

Regarding the identity of Mystery Babylon, although I have read what you have written carefully regarding your belief that Mystery Babylon represents all denominational churches with the Roman Catholic Church being the figurehead, I remain unconvinced for a number of reasons. Most of these reasons I have already shared with you in my previous letter. But, to recap briefly: (a) there are strong arguments made by Christians for Mystery Babylon being Communism, Islam, the United States, etc., (b) the accuracy of the classic work you have referred to several times by Alex Hislop, that is, *The Two Babylons*, is questionable on historical and methodological grounds, (c) the powerful ways God is currently working through denominations through program-based or cell group-based structures, (d) the evangelical and charismatic renewal movements that are occurring across all denominational barriers and in the larger body of Christ whether Catholic, Orthodox, Anglican, Protestant, Independent, etc, (e) the way God has worked through the church in history through denominational people like John Wesley, Count Zinzendorf, Ulrich Zwingli, Martin Luther, D.L. Moody, Charles Spurgeon, Charles Finney, Jonathan Edwards, William Booth, etc., and (f) my own personal experience working for a dozen years with a denominational church and missions organizations like Campus Crusade for Christ and The Navigators. Remember, a denomination and many denominational friends and relatives are actually supporting in various ways our house church efforts here. For these reasons, let me state clearly, I do not believe that non-house church Christ-followers are part of Mystery Babylon. You have failed to convince me about your strongly held conviction, just as I have failed to convince you about my conviction. All that we can do is to be true to our conscience, Scripture, and the Spirit. I will not and cannot act contrary to any of these. So, at this point, I do not see any reason to continue detailed communications and debates on this particular issue. Further in depth analysis, I'm afraid, will be fruitless for both of us. I do not want to spend any more of your time or my time on this, when the work of prayer, discipleship, and evangelism is ever increasingly upon us and is far more important. This is my posture, and it will stay this way in the days ahead.

My attitude towards the denominational churches and missions organizations is that God is doing a big work through them. Most other house church people I have met share this same attitude. Remember, most of the house church activity going on all over the world is often sponsored by denominations and missions groups or at least was started by them. Jesus loves his church. As such, Jesus encourages and criticizes his church. That is fine. This is as it should be. But you and I must be extremely careful in our criticisms. May I say that, in fighting against the denominations and other believers working within them, take care that you do not find yourself fighting against God. Be sure you know with certainty that the Lord is leading you in your criticisms of other parts of the Body of Christ. I agree with a wise old Pharisee in my attitude to others who love the Lord and are doing his work, even though I don't necessarily agree with everything they do or believe: "But a Pharisee named Gamaliel, a teacher of the law, who was honored by all the people, stood up in the Sanhedrin and ordered that the men be put outside for a little while. Then he addressed them: 'Men of Israel, consider carefully what you intend to do to these men. Therefore, in the present case I advise you: Leave these men alone! Let them go! For if their purpose or activity is of human origin, it will fail. But if it is from God, you will not be able to stop these men; you will only find yourselves fighting against God.'" (Acts 5:34,35,38,39 NIV). Consequently, my attitude and practice is one of reform and renewal (as was John Wesley's and many other great men of God in history as you know from your study of the church) and not reaction, and will be so in the days to come. Whenever I am able to help a traditional program-based church with no small groups develop a small groups ministry, I will do so. And I have done that for two churches and am helping a third one right now. Whenever a church with a small groups ministry desires to take the next step and transition into a pure cell-group-based model, I will help where I can. Whenever a cell church desires to take the next step and sell its building and reorganize into house churches, I will help where I can too. These are all tough and brave steps to take that, I believe, God is involved in. I want to partner with God and his people and not try to push God or people into my timeframe of doing things. In all of these situations, though, I will talk to people about house churches and the improvements needed within the institutional churches. I believe it is better that some changes are made, step by step, than that no changes are ever made because a sudden change to a house church model is too big a mental and structural leap for many. I want to help move people and churches along the spectrum towards a more biblical model, step by step, in a pace they can handle. Where they decide to stop in that process is between them and God. God is their judge, not me. This is my attitude and practice and it will stay this way in the foreseeable future.

Regarding the two of us working together, obviously, we have some divergence on these points. On the practical level of working together, these are serious barriers, as you also pointed out. I do not consider you unsaved or a heathen or anything of that sort. My friend and I are sure you know the Lord and love him with your heart and deeply desire to follow his will and experience him in your life. We are glad about that. However, to be open and honest, we are concerned about your views and the resulting practices you carry out regarding Mystery Babylon, denominations, and mission organizations. We feel they sometimes cross onto dangerous, unhealthy, and biblically questionable grounds. As elders, we will not endorse these views and teachings to the people God has currently put under our care (a number of whom are very tender in their faith) or in future house churches related to our ministry. Nor do we desire to bring in teachers who will advocate these views into our midst. So, for the time being, because you advocate these views very strongly and urgently (out of a sincere conscience), we cannot by our own good conscience invite you to bring such teachings to our group. We want to be friends, meet together, eat together, perhaps even have our families meet informally, but we need to work through these issues (if that is possible) for us to have anything like a real working ministry relationship or for mutual visits when the church gathers. You may have the same stance towards us in inviting us to teach or speak to your group given our differing attitude towards denominations and the larger Body of Christ. I believe this is wise on both sides for the time being.

    Allow me now to make a proposal. I do not think these issues will be sorted out any time soon if at all. I don't think that my friend nor I nor our house church will come to your understanding just given a little more time. We do not hold these views or interpretations of Scripture and they will not change in the foreseeable future. If you think they will change if you "work with us" a little more, you may find yourself quite frustrated unnecessarily. I propose that you do not frustrate yourself further by expecting or pushing us to come to your understanding of Scripture regarding denominations, Mystery Babylon, other Christians like Billy Graham and John Wesley, etc. We do not agree from our conscience, reason, experience, Scripture, and the Spirit. We believe God is working in a variety of ways today as he has in the past. I also propose that our working relationship for the time being consist basically of meeting from time to time casually and informally (say over lunch at a coffee shop or restaurant) to encourage, pray for each other in the work we are doing with our current house churches, and to exchange resources. Perhaps this is like Paul and Peter giving each other the right hand of fellowship and recognizing that each of them have different fields of ministry. This is the extent of working together that I foresee in the near future. Would you be open to reading a short book or listening to an audio tape by a well-known Catholic priest, Henri Nouwen, on the spiritual life and what it means to walk with Christ?

    Well brother, that brings me to the close of this letter. I would like to hear specifically what you feel about the above three practical proposals.

With sincerity in Christ,
Rad Zdero

Letter #3
This letter was my next contribution sent to the same gentleman as above in Letter #1 and #2. At this point I felt we had discussed certain issues as much as we could. The question was whether we could work together practically in starting and visiting house churches.

Hello again Brother,
    I did receive your entire email and read through it. Obviously much thought and heart went into it. Truly, thanks for your genuineness in this. I will respond briefly to your email at a couple of larger and more encompassing points.
    Let me say, you pointed out you felt I was "tossed to and fro" by every wind of doctrine and that's why I was accepting of many Christians and the way I see God working clearly in missions groups and throughout history, etc. It is just the opposite. It is because I do not fall easy prey to every idea or whim that comes along, that I have not simply accepted and agreed with everything you have said. You should not be amazed that I do not become so easily swayed by your quotes from books or authorities, no matter how seemingly convincing they are to others. Whenever I have made any great shifts in paradigm, then it has come through a long process of thought, study, and prayer, and will not occur over the space of a few e-mails, however long, and conversations. This, as a brother, you are getting to know about me. You are quite mistaken when you say I do not have a view yet. Quite the contrary. My view I have clearly spelled out regarding the nature of God's work throughout history, specifically regarding the role of renewal and reform movements within the church. Understanding how God works is not simply limited to acquiring an accurate knowledge of the Bible. God has imbued within us our conscience, the Spirit, reason, and experience. Because I do not hammer on you with my convictions does not mean that they are not firm ones. I see, too, that you are resolute in your convictions about various items and no doubt this has come to you through many hours of thought, sleepless nights, prayer, and study. I believe we are very similar in this regard, and that is why we have been able to have

such an ongoing conversation. Am I guessing correctly when I say that perhaps you have not had many co-pilgrims along this long road to such a degree? Most people, I imagine, have not had the patience nor tolerance to engage things to this degree with you over the years.

Regarding the Roman Catholic Church, perhaps there is a lack of understanding here in our communication. I do not suggest that the Roman Catholic Church is in no way connected to Mystery Babylon. I do see that there is a connection. There is biblical and historic precedent. And I am quite aware that many a Christian has viewed the Roman Catholic Church this way. I am suggesting that it is perhaps one of many possibilities of connection, as is Islam, Communism, the United States, the ancient Roman Empire, and the revived Roman Empire to come. All of these may have some connection to Mystery Babylon, but the details of which seem unclear to me because of the sometimes shaky methodology of "parallelism" employed by proponents who espouse 100% certainty. Parallelism can and has been used to justify all sorts of things throughout history, even horrendous things within the church (e.g. Abraham has many wives so it's okay for Mormons to do so; Abraham had slaves so we can justify American slavery; David went to war and Joshua was commanded to clear the land so we now have a "just war" theory). This is especially the case when it has come to prophecy. You, I'm sure, are well aware of the millennium craze that happened in the year 1000 AD in Europe, or in the Middle Ages when the Black Plague came along, or even during World War 2 with Christians identifying Hitler and Mussolini as the False Prophet and the Anti-Christ. Many books have been written about such things. However, they were all wrong despite the many parallels that the authors were able to muster. Parallels can be found between any two things if we try hard enough and if we have the mindset. For example, key words like "harlot", "seven", "purple", etc., have been used in arguing the USA is Mystery Babylon and other theories. So, when the writings of authors are offered (most of whom are Protestants for whom anti-Romanism is fashionable in their circles, or are pseudo-Christian cultists) who hold that the Roman

Catholic Church is definitely Mystery Babylon, of course I am cautious and slow about embracing the idea. I am not closed to it, I just remain unconvinced and take a "wait and see" and "study and pray and think some more" attitude about it all. Let me state again as I did in my previous email, that it seems fruitless for us to engage in any more great detail about this topic of secondary importance for now. Another 20-page email on the topic will not adequately address things. This is bearing no fruit for either of us.

Regarding cells and John Wesley, it is clear to me that God used John Wesley and the 10,000 cell groups he established (which functioned more like open meetings), to mark a milestone in the history of the church. Let me be blunt here. I would rather see a thriving cell group ministry (which you see as unbiblical) with many people coming to know Christ and with an ever expanding circle of disciples, than one or two floundering house churches who are convinced of being the only "biblical" Christians but who are not doing much of anything. When and if you and I are used by God to spawn house churches that seem to bear much good fruit, as the Bible commands, then perhaps we have something significant to share with others about the cell church versus house church debate. My conviction is that small discipleship circles, as modeled by Jesus and the 12, are the most effective way to be the church to each other. In this regard, if God called me to be a prophetic voice of change in the institutional church (as John Wesley was) by reforming church structure into cells and small groups and house churches, rather than leaving, of course I would do it. Personally, I have no huge desire to go into the institutions to do so, but am willing to work with those who are part of them to see such changes take place. That perhaps clarifies my position.

Regarding the next steps in our communication, for me the Babylon issue is a distraction from the more important ones. How about we address the following? The issues I would like to talk with you more about from a biblical standpoint are cells vs. house churches, reform / renewal vs. leaving the institutional church, church leadership, etc. This is far more critical to reaching our cities with the great news of Jesus. Would you be up for changing the course of our email conversations from Mystery Babylon to this instead? I see this being more fruitful. I will also pass on a brief Henri Nouwen tape to you called "Who are we? Our identity in Christ." It may actually be beneficial spiritually. I personally have no doubt that Henri was a genuine man of God. By the way, I still have some of your audio tapes that I should return.

Finally, I do not wish to separate from you over this Mystery Babylon issue at all. If this is your conviction about Mystery Babylon being the Roman Catholic Church, that's fine. If what you have communicated to our mutual friend is that I want to part ways over this, you have probably innocently miscommunicated my intentions. My point in the last email was that I do not wish, nor do I think it is biblical, that this Mystery Babylon issue become the over-riding issue in our conversations or in the house church(es) related to the ministry God has given to my friend and me. There are far more vital issues like prayer, discipleship, evangelism, and helping the poor and lonely. This is the crux of the New Testament church's activity, not the identity of Mystery Babylon. I do not want to become an unbalanced or lopsided Christian or house church, which focuses unbiblically too much on one topic, whatever the topic might be. This is my concern in working with you closely in ministry. Am I misunderstanding you? Please clarify this.

All for now brother. Take good care.
Breathe deep the breath of God,
Rad Zdero

Letter #4

The following letter was my final one written to the same house church elder from Letter #1, #2, and #3. Although I liked him personally, there were big philosophical challenges that prevented us from partnering together. Eventually, I decided not to work together with him, but I held no hard feelings towards him and continued to be friendly in any subsequent interactions we may have had.

Hi Brother,

I hope this note finds you, your family, and your ministry doing well. The reason I'm writing instead of making a telephone call, is that hand written letters these days are a dying art form, something I hope to remedy in my own life anyway. And I wanted to follow up on our last conversations we have had and not allow things to just slip away. I have been processing things and feel I have come to some conclusions I wish to share with you. Please know that my intentions and attitude toward you are sincere and in good faith.

Regarding personal friendship, for the most part, I have enjoyed our interactions over lunch, over email, and otherwise. I hope we can continue to be in touch from time to time to catch up and encourage one another. You and I have processed many ideas and navigated some tensions, I think for our mutual benefit. What maintaining contact looks like is something we will need to play by ear. However, I do know that I need to focus particularly on those friendships that are immediately around me and the people with whom I am building.

With respect to theological issues, you and I have worked through a number of topics and ideas around the Christian life and ministry. It is clear we have overlap and agreement and some disagreement too. That's okay with me. However, at this point I do not feel the need and the desire, nor do I have the energy to work through life and ministry issues with you in detail, beyond what we have done already. We had started working through eldership and itinerant workers with some agreement and disagreement. I think we have to leave things where they are and agree to disagree on some of those things, respecting each other as we do.

Now, about starting house churches together, you have suggested that we could work together to start home meetings in partnership. In principle, I am open to this, but am concerned that our differing understandings of properly applying the Scriptures to various issues would prevent this from being practical and realistic. These issues, as you know, revolve around women in leadership, attitudes towards traditional and cell group churches, baptism, the Lord's Supper, open meetings versus several brothers doing all the talking, etc. If you have any ideas as to how we could actually start a house church together and build it up despite these differences, I am open to hear it. However, to me it seems we would be at odds on these items, making working together very impractical in the long run.

All for now and all the best in Christ,
Rad Zdero

6

LETTERS TO CRITICS OF HOUSE CHURCHES

Letter #1

This letter was sent in response to a person who wrote a paper reviewing my book The Global House Church Movement. Their main contention was that the New Testament's primary ecclesiological structure was not the house church, but rather the city church. Our exchange was pleasant and respectful.

Dear Friend,

    I hope you are well. Thanks for the opportunity to respond to your review of chapter 3 ("Biblical Foundations: Church, First-Century Style") of my book *The Global House Church Movement* (2004). I have read it and found it very interesting. I agree with many points you make. To be honest, though, I also disagree with many other points and feel your essay sometimes misrepresents or does not mention what I actually wrote in my book. Even so, I am glad to be in dialogue with a fellow Christian like you who studies the Scriptures carefully and wishes to apply it to their life. I hope that you will consider attaching my response letter to your review, if you have plans of posting it on the web or circulating it to your readers. This, I think, would be only fair and would promote good dialogue between well-meaning Christians who are seeking to impact the world for Christ. There are only several points I would like to respond to, since this would otherwise be a much longer document if I tried to address every point you raised. Thank you again for the opportunity to dialogue and to let "iron sharpen iron."

Bible Scholars and the Early House Churches

It is a well-accepted idea among biblical scholars today that the early church of the first three centuries AD was indeed a house-based movement. This is no longer a matter of debate in the academic community and has been recognized for a number of years. Part of this was due to cultural patterns and the centrality of the "household" or "family" in the early centuries, which the Christians used strategically in their village-reaching and city-reaching efforts. New Testament Professor Roger Gehring, in his 2004 landmark book *House Church and Mission: The Importance of Household Structures in Early Christianity*, informs us that, "On one point nearly all NT scholars presently agree: early Christians met almost exclusively in the homes of individual members of the congregation. For nearly three hundred years— until the fourth century, when Constantine began building the first basilicas throughout the Roman Empire—Christians gathered in private houses built initially for domestic use, not in church buildings originally constructed for the sole purpose of public worship" (Gehring, *House Church and Mission*, page 1).

My short book was only meant to be a brief overview of the biblical, historical, and practical aspects of the house church movement and, as such, there may be some gaps in it. It was not meant to be an in-depth analysis of everything on the matter, nor was it meant to clarify in great detail every point that could possibly be raised. For a detailed scholarly analysis of New Testament church patterns, I think you would appreciate reading the following material written by New Testament scholars, such as Roger Gehring, *House Church and Mission: The Importance of Household Structures in Early Christianity* (2004), Robert Banks,

Paul's Idea of Community: The Early House Churches in their Cultural Setting (1994), Vincent Branick, *The House Church in the Writings of Paul* (1989), Del Birkey, *The House Church: A Model for Renewing the Church* (1988), B.B. Blue, "Acts and the House Church," in *The Book of Acts in Its Graeco-Roman Setting*, D.W.J. Gill and C. Gempf (eds.), 1994, pages 119-222, and Floyd Filson, "The Significance of the Early House Churches," *Journal of Biblical Literature*, 1939, vol.58, pp.105-112.

Houses and Households in the New Testament

In several places, your essay makes statements similar to this one: "...if the house church is such an important New Testament concept, and if it is true that believers met primarily in homes, why is reference to this so scanty?" Specifically, you suggest that there are only four references in which the word "church" (Greek = *ekklesia*) is connected directly to meeting in a home (Rom 16:5; 1 Cor 16:19; Col 4:15; Philem 1:2). I would like you to consider the following.

In the New Testament writings, the word *ekklesia* does not have to be explicitly mentioned every single time to indicate that a legitimate believers' church meeting is happening. Why? The word "house" (Greek = *oikia*) or "household" (Greek = *oikos*) in the New Testament means "abode, family, dwelling, home, house" (Strong's Exhaustive Concordance). An *oikia* or *oikos* would include the immediate family members, servants, and friends associated socially with the house or household. At that time in history, a person's home was often the center of their social and economic activity. The "household" (Greek = *oikos*), therefore, was a natural context for the religious activity of Christians. Roger Gehring, professor of New Testament studies, once again observes that there was "an integration of the Christian community with the social and economic infrastructure of the ancient *oikos*" (Gehring, *House Church and Mission*, page 291). It was therefore natural that, "Houses also served as bases of operations and meeting places for prayer, table fellowship, and teaching in the missional outreach of Jesus' disciples. Later, in the primitive church in Jerusalem, houses were used for assembly, community formation and fellowship, prayer, teaching, and the celebration of the Lord's Supper. It is legitimate here to speak of house churches as churches in the full sense, as all of the ecclesiological elements that constitute the church are observable...This use of houses is continued then in Antioch and in all phases of the Pauline mission." (Gehring, *House Church and Mission*, page 295).

Therefore, whenever we see believers meeting in a "house" or as a "household" in the New Testament, they were inevitably engaged in some form of spiritual activity, like prayer, teaching, eating, encouraging, and even evangelizing and healing people. And there are many such references to spiritual activities by Jesus and the apostles in the "house" and the "household", such as Mark 1:29-34, 2:1-2, 14:13-16, Luke 10:1-11, Acts 2:46, 5:42, 10:1-48, 12:12, 16:14-15, 18:7-11, 20:6-8,20, Rom 16:5, 1 Cor 16:15,19, Col 4:15, and Philem 1:2. Whether the word *ekklesia* is specifically mentioned or not when believers met as a "household" is not really the point. The point is that they were gathering together and functioning as a spiritual family (i.e. a church) in the context of their homes, as well as other places.

Today's House Church Movement Is More Than Just Meeting in Houses

Throughout your review, unfortunately, it seems there is a misunderstanding of my book *The Global House Church Movement* and the house church movement in general by implying that we are arguing for meeting in private houses only, and that large public meetings are not important. This is not correct, as I say very often in my book. For the house church, the small group of believers is the important part, not the physical house. This is the primary basic unit because it is one's spiritual family, where you can have the personal deep relationships, accountability, teaching, and support that you cannot get if you are always just in a large group setting, like many modern traditional churches try to do. But the house church (i.e. small group) must never be isolated and must function in networks of house churches at the city church level (Acts 20:20).

More specifically, I mention many times in my book that the house church movement is not just about meeting in private houses. For example, in my book I wrote, "To network together, these house churches meet house-to-house, organize citywide events for teaching and worship, and have mobile workers that circulate from group-to-group and city-to-city like blood through arteries." (Zdero, *The Global House Church Movement*, page 3). I also write entire sections in my book about how house churches should work together practically in networks and to meet at the city level publicly for various purposes, for evangelism as well as teaching and worship (page 84, 106-109, 114-115, 129).

Specifically, in my analysis of the New Testament in chapter 3 of my book, I mention this: "The record shows that all individual believers and house churches considered themselves as part of a single citywide church. As such, for both Jewish and Gentile Christians, citywide gatherings were employed as part of the experience of being a Christian and as an expression of unity with other believers." (Zdero, *The Global House Church Movement*, page 51). I also write entire sections on pages 22-23 and 49-52 showing how the house churches in the New Testament were connected together into a larger movement and into citywide networks, where "they may have all gathered together as a larger body from time to time in some open field, on a hillside, or in a rented space, for a specific decision-making purpose... and also gather all the house church elders in the that city from some sort of public endeavor, either for an evangelistic purpose or for training." (Zdero, *The Global House Church Movement*, page 52).

The Word "Church" (Greek = *Ekklesia*) in the New Testament

You point out that, on page 18 of my book, I mention that the word "church" (Greek = *ekklesia*) appears 114 times. You do a good job of providing a more detailed analysis showing that most of the uses of the word *ekklesia* in the New Testament refer to the "city" (72 times) or "universal" (16 times) church or other types, rather than for the "house" church (4 times). Your conclusion is that, "Considering this fact, it is not so difficult to see the church assembling in large groups and not only in small groups in the confines of private homes." I agree with this conclusion in general. However, I would like to clarify several items about your analysis and conclusions.

Allow me to suggest that you are incorrectly assuming that when a church at the city level is mentioned, that this almost always means that there were a large number of Christians in that city. It must be remembered, however, that for Paul, each city had just one church, whether there were few or many believers, whether they met in a house or outside or somewhere else. Some cities only had one small house church, which happened especially when the gospel was first planted in a new place. For example, the new church meeting at Lydia's home in the city of Thyatira was composed of people connected to her "household." (Acts 16:14-15). Based on Paul's previous habit, this one house church (whether 3 people or 30 people) would then be viewed as the "church of Thyatira." The fact that the city church is mentioned 72 times, actually tells us nothing about the total number of believers in each of those cities, whether few or many. In most cases, we cannot tell for sure and must look case by case at each Scripture.

We must also remember that the homes of non-believers became the natural place where the church would meet when the householders became believers. There is no evidence that the apostles permanently took these new believers from their household to only meet in a special building. Specifically, you mention Acts 5:42, 16:14-15, and 20:20 as being only for evangelistic ministry, not for churches. This is only partially true. There is always some overlap between preaching to non-believers and teaching for believers. For example, when Peter visited the large group of people in Cornelius' home in Acts 10:1-11:21, he went there to preach evangelistically. Then, the Holy Spirit fell on the group before Peter was even finished speaking about Christ, showing that they now had come to faith in Christ (Acts 10:44). Before Peter came, a church was not there in the home. After Peter came, a church was started in that home. This one household church (whether 3 people or 30 people) was now, therefore, by definition the church of the city of Caesarea. The same can be said for Luke 10:1-11, Acts 5:42, 16:14-15, 16:30-34, 18:7-8, 20:20, 28:30 and many other scriptures. By the way, this "man of peace" or "house of peace" strategy is exactly how many thousands of house churches are started today in Burma, Cuba, Philippines, India, China, etc.

Apostolic Blueprint in the New Testament

In your essay, you suggest that apostolic "traditions are personal ways of thinking and behaving. To read into the word the practice of meeting in houses is simply too much, and I might add, a little bit ludicrous." I will only respond to this very briefly by suggesting the following.

First, I never suggest in my book that meeting in a physical house is the main point of the "traditions" of the apostles. Far from it. I was careful to qualify the role of the physical house in my book, when I wrote that, "Although they did not necessarily employ the house church form consciously, it was the natural result of their theology of church as family and their belief in the participatory and interactive nature of gatherings." (Zdero, *The Global House Church Movement*, page 56).

Second, to suggest that it is "ludicrous" that there is a kind of pattern or "tradition" for the church to follow is to ignore the many able theologians and scholars and movements throughout history that have believed that indeed there are patterns in the New Testament for the church to follow. I would direct you to read the works of the Anabaptists/Mennonites, the Quakers, the Brethren, etc.

Third, there are many "traditions" that the church has indeed been faithful to follow. Baptizing new believers by water as an expression of their new faith is a tradition. Meeting regularly together as believers is a tradition. The Lord's Supper is a tradition. Whether we realize it or not, we all follow some types of traditions in our churches. The challenge is to discern New Testament traditions and apply them today.

Fourth, I see no reason for limiting the "traditions" of the apostles in 1 Cor 11:2 and 2 Thes 2:15 to merely personal ways of thinking and behaving. These letters were addressed to churches and, as such, certainly are to be taken personally, but also apply to corporate life. We are not told in the Scripture that we are to follow God only as individual believers, but also as a corporate body.

Fifth, please consider Paul's statements that "whatever you have learned or received or heard from me, or seen in me—put into practice. And the God of peace will be with you." (Philip 4:9 NIV) and that Timothy "will remind you of my ways which are in Christ, just as I teach everywhere in every church." (1 Cor 4:17 NASB). Is Paul really only speaking about personal morality, or is he talking about that, plus other matters that pertain to the mission of the church?

Sixth, I would encourage you to read the chapter by Steve Atkerson entitled "The Authority of Apostolic Tradition in the New Testament era" (pages 151-157) in my new book *Nexus: The World House Church Movement Reader* (2007) available from www.MissionBooks.org. Also, there is a similar article on Steve Atkerson's website www.ntrf.org. These articles go into much more detail on apostolic traditions than I could in the short book of mine that you reviewed.

The Role of Small Groups and Large Groups in the Church Today

In several places, you make statements like these: "involved a sizable number of believers"; "there seemed to be houses big enough to accommodate large numbers of people"; "an essential feature of the life of the early believers is constantly being together. They met daily in big, citywide, all believers, public, church meetings. And they met separately in private homes." I am happy that you have identified elements that are crucial for today's church in reaching the world for Christ. I would like to make some comments.

First, from my own practical experience, from church history, and from the New Testament, I suggest that there needs to be a healthy emphasis on small groups and large groups. This is something I have discussed in my book in many places. More specifically, what I mean is the need for both the small group and the city church. Each has their strength. The small group—whether it meets in a house or not is really not the point—is great at mutual accountability, mutual teaching, mutual prayer, mutual sharing, and even evangelism. The city church—which I suggest quite literally means all believers in the city gathering together—is good for cross-pollination, teamwork, training, evangelism, worship, teaching, etc. Although the New Testament shows the small group (in the form of the private house church) and the large group (in the form of the public city church), the modern church often does not do either adequately. Instead, the modern church often uses the mid-sized group called the "congregation", which has its own building that usually contains no more than several hundred people. Anyone who has been a Christian for some time or is actively involved in leadership, recognizes that the mid-sized "congregation" cannot, on its own, adequately achieve either the discipleship that a small group can, or the celebration that citywide church meetings can. Perhaps we should go to a model that replaces the mid-sized "congregation" with a more New Testament approach using "living rooms" (i.e. the small group) and "stadiums" (i.e. the city church). This is, in fact, the direction in which much of the house church movement is going.

Second, statistics for today's church show some interesting things. The fastest growing church planting movements around the world utilize house churches of between 10 to 30 members. See the book by well-known missiologist David Garrison entitled *Church Planting Movements*, which documents this clearly. From 1998 to 2006, an estimated 300,000 new house churches have started globally, as noted by Wolfgang Simson in *The Starfish Manifesto* (www.StarfishPortal.net). This number does not include what is happening in China with 80 to 100 million believers in house churches, or the 1 million house church-type groups in Latin America called Basic Christian Communities. In America, 75% of churches are not growing numerically at all, 24% of churches are growing numerically only by Christians migrating from one church to another church, while only 1% of churches are growing through seeing new people come to faith, as noted in my book *Nexus: The World House Church Movement*

Reader on page 458. Only 1% of people who come to faith in Christ in large evangelistic crusade meetings get connected to a congregation, as reported by Wolfgang Simson in *Houses that Change the World* on page 199. Given these points, allow me to propose that the global church needs to become more strategic and more focused in the use of small groups in gathering and nurturing new believers, whether through cell groups or house churches. Thanks again brother for the opportunity to respond. May the Lord prosper your body, your soul, and your ministry.

With kindest regards,
Rad Zdero

Letter #2
The following is only an excerpt from a much longer letter I wrote to provide chapter-by-chapter feedback to an author who wrote an unpublished draft manuscript about various movements within the church. In the book, he heavily criticized the house church movement in the West and suggested that house churches in China were only a default position due to persecution. The excerpt below is my response to his view of house churches. My complete response letter was received gratefully by him.

Dear Brother,
 This is an excellent work by a well-informed influencer. Broad scope. Easy to read. Enjoyable. The analysis is mostly balanced, but a few chapters require more pros or cons for a given church stream. Some chapters would improve with more Scripture references, so the critique is principle-based, not preference-based. This is a worthy addition to the library of any practitioner and student of missiology. I hope to get my own copy when published. Several comments can be made here.
 First, almost an entire chapter is dedicated to pointing out the weaknesses of house churches in the West, but a fair analysis must include the strengths also. A subsection outlining the strengths of the house church movement would go a long way to help properly

present this stream. The reader is left wondering if there is some unstated reason on the part of the author for this approach.

Second, I know of no house church leaders in the West that do not participate, or refuse to participate on principle, in some form of large group gathering, even if it is only several house churches meeting occasionally in a large home. Certainly, there are always people on the fringe of movements, including the house church movement, that are anomalies. But, it is inaccurate for the reader to be left with the impression that house churches in the West think large group gatherings are irrelevant at best or evil at worst. This simply is not the case. Wolfgang Simson, Neil Cole, Frank Viola, Robert Fitts, Tony Dale, Felicity Dale, Steve Atkerson, Larry Kreider, and many others including myself all advocate for the appropriate and strategic use of large group settings, etc, whether in a large home, a community center, a big conference hall, or even sometimes in an existing church building. Please see my *The Global House Church Movement* (pages 22, 23, 50-52, 106-109) and *Nexus: The World House Church Movement Reader* (pages 126-128, 421-422, 512-513). To re-iterate, for example, the autonomous house churches in our Canadian network use larger gatherings often for conferences, retreats, camp-outs, think tanks, and training seminars, as "macro" supplements to the "micro" house units. Personally, one of my roles in my immediate region is to interconnect the "micro" and "macro" and to encourage autonomous house churches to form citywide networks (Acts 20:17,20).

Third, I think the misunderstanding among some critics of house churches may be that, for most house churches, the "network" functions as the large group wing, unlike the cell church in which a well-defined "congregation" dimension is the large group wing. Your earlier observation applies here and should be made much more explicit.

Fourth, the Scriptures from the Book of Acts offered to support the "congregation" dimension are what house church leaders term the citywide house church network, once the context of each of the Scriptures is closely examined. Ironically, you earlier criticize one house church writer for advocating the citywide network idea. This should be clarified and presented in a more precise way.

It may be just a matter of different terminology and timing (e.g. weekly, monthly, bi-monthly, yearly) between cell churches and house church networks in their need or desire for the large group wing in the West.

Fifth, phrases like so-and-so is "blind" and house church leaders in the West are "blinded" should be softened, as they will not help in the reconciling intentions of the book.

Sixth, as a point of interest, statistically speaking, house churches are among the most effective evangelistic churches in the West. A major survey by professor J.D. Payne in his book *Missional House Churches* (2008) examined house churches in America that were "missional", being defined as those groups that had planted at least 1 other house church in the previous 3 years and had baptized at least 1 new believer in the past 1 year. About 24% to 43% of the members in these house churches were brand new believers. This is in stark contrast to the net loss being experienced by mainstream churches of 48 congregations every week (Larry Kreider, *House Church Networks*, page 67).

Finally, regarding your chapter on the house churches in China, some Scriptures would be helpful in the analysis. It should also be noted clearly that some of the major streams of Chinese house churches comprising millions of believers wish to retain a "tabernacle", rather than a "temple", church mentality even if full blown political openness comes to the country, and for mission work outside the country. They have decided (a) not to construct buildings, (b) only financially support traveling evangelists and missionaries while local leaders remain unpaid volunteers, (c) model teamwork, and (d) not allow any one leader to stay too long in one place lest it create unhealthy dependency. So, it is perhaps not accurate to suggest that the house church strategy is merely a default scenario for the Chinese. See Larry Kreider's *House Church Networks* (page 41-42), Paul Hattaway's *Back to Jerusalem*, and Rad Zdero's *Nexus: The World House Church Movement Reader* (chapter 28).

With best regards,
Rad Zdero

Letter #3

This letter was send to a former traditional pastor who was not involved in the house church movement, but was morally supportive of it. He sent me a quick note expressing his concern that a well-known house church ministry was asking for financial help to move forward in their efforts. Although gentle and genuine in his criticism of that ministry, I felt that I should respond with a few remarks that might clarify the issue of money for mission in the house church movement.

Hi Brother,

Thanks for pointing out the website to which you were referring about your worry that a particular house church ministry was requesting financial donations. If I understand your prior note to me, your concern is that house churches do not go back to an institutional church, or "old wineskin", approach by becoming too dependent on, or even asking for, money for their mission. I'd like to make just a few quick remarks about this important topic.

First, I read through the website you mentioned, and I don't generally have any big problem with how they made their financial needs known to those who may be led by God to help out. However, if any house churches or house church networks use any kind of pressure tactics, including trying to enforce a mandatory giving policy, then I would be very concerned. Then I would agree with you that an "old wineskin" mentality has crept in and should be clearly addressed and changed.

Second, I think there is an incorrect assumption out there that, because house churches do not have paid pastors or facility costs or expensive programs, no finances are ever needed at all. In more institutional churches, as you know, typical budgets are divided up into 80% for staff salaries and the church building, while only about 20% goes directly to internal ministry or external mission. But for a typical network of house churches, the numbers are probably reversed with about 20% going to renting a place for a conference, celebration, weekend retreat, supporting a traveling apostolic worker, etc, while about 80% goes to resources like buying Bibles, running websites, producing magazines, supporting soup kitchens, helping homeless shelters, etc. I'd have to do a deeper research study on this to get more accurate numbers.

Third, allow me to give a practical example. In the regional and national house church conferences I help organize in Canada, I always get a comment from someone saying that, in principle, there should be no registration fee for participants because it is a Christian event. In their view, it is somehow unspiritual and unscriptural to have a registration fee. Yet, I always have to remind people that it is unfair for the conference organizing team to be saddled with the cost of the entire event, since there are financial costs associated with facility rental, meals, post-event cleaning staff, audiovisual recording, etc. Even if an offering were taken by passing a basket around, it may not meet the need. Then the organizing team, who would not want to pass the basket around a second time for fear of being accused of greed, would get stuck with the bill. Often I think people who have never organized an event really don't realize all the costs involved. As the saying goes, there is no free lunch, whether you are in an institutional church or a house church network. However, I do believe the house church movement is much more strategic and effective in its use of funds than institutional churches.

Fourth, I have written on the topic of finances in the house church movement in my books and in the *Starfish Files* magazine, as well as having talked with several trusted peers about the issue. Some people in house churches do not want to speak or write about the issue publicly for fear of their motivations being wrongly interpreted. Why? Because there is still an unhealthy and immature reactionary tendency in some groups to anything that even remotely reminds them of their past experience in the institutional church, such as money for ministry. Yet, I believe, we need to recapture a healthy biblical understanding and use of money for mission as we see in the New Testament. I don't want to see a situation where some things God wants accomplished don't get done because of an immature and unscriptural attitude about giving. In our Canadian network, we are turning a corner on this by maturely, prayerfully, and scripturally mobilizing funds where needed or at least letting people know about various needs across the network. We do not teach mandatory tithing and so all of the giving is voluntary and without compulsion.

Fifth, I am personally not interested in either rebelling against or upholding the institutional church's practices with respect to money. I am interested in what the Scripture says and allowing the Spirit to guide me to deal with on-the-ground circumstances. What do I see in Scripture? Basically, local leaders – who were interchangeably called elders/presbyters, pastors/shepherds, or overseers/bishops – were not supported financially for their ministry, but were encouraged to use their own finances to help others in the church (Acts 20:33-35). There was no need to give them salaries because an unpaid small team of multiple elders/leaders (Acts 14:23; Rom 16:3-5; James 5:14; 1 Tim 4:14) could easily lead a New Testament-era house church, which usually had at most 30 to 35 people according to the archaeological data (Del Birkey, *The House Church*, Herald Press, 1988, p.55). However, if someone wanted to give a gift to an elder, that was certainly acceptable (Gal 6:6). Any money and resources voluntarily collected in the New Testament house churches were used to help support the poor and needy (Acts 2:44-45; Acts 11:29; 1 Cor 16:1-3), as well as apostles who travelled widely, started new churches, grouped them into networks, visited them on occasion, and moved on to repeat the process (Luke 10:1-9; 1 Cor 9:1-15; Philip 4:15-19; 3 John 1:5-8). This is how many exploding house church movements are functioning, like our Chinese and Indian friends who funnel finances to travelling evangelists and apostles for outward kingdom expansion, rather than local leaders or facilities.

Finally, thanks for considering this all too brief treatise on money and mission with respect to the emerging house church movement. I'd be happy to know what your thoughts are on the matter.

Pax Christi,
Rad Zdero

Letter #4

This letter was written on a public internet blog in response to remarks left by a gentleman who had once asked me a question in a seminar about whether house churches need to get together regularly in a large group setting. His point was that large group gatherings were encouraging and exciting and should be used by house churches. Apparently he felt I did not consider his ideas carefully enough in my response to him at the seminar and, therefore, I wanted to clarify my position to him and others in this public forum.

Dear Friends,

I am responding to the comment made by the brother about house churches and large group meetings. I am sad to hear that he felt I "brushed him aside" in my response about house churches and small groups. I certainly would not have done so deliberately. I try to take all questions posed to me seriously. My whole point was that large group events — in and of themselves — are not absolutely necessary for house churches to keep growing, like they grow in many parts of the world without frequent large group meetings.

Moreover, sometimes large group events can be negative factors, if they are not used properly since, as anyone who has been around the block knows, they often breed a spectator church experience if attendees are not also involved in an interactive small group or house church. How often a network of house churches decides to meet as a large group is up to them and their perceived needs and how God leads them, whether weekly, monthly, or yearly. In Canada, we use large group gatherings often, such as weekend retreats, campouts, conferences, regional meetings, etc.

In my books *The Global House Church Movement* and *Nexus: The World House Church Movement Reader*, I explain in a number of places that large group gatherings have their strategic use for house churches. So, it is not true that I am against large group meetings of multiple house churches. But, large group meet-ups should not become the main ingredient for a Christian's experience in place of the small group, like it does unfortunately in many traditional churches. Of course, all this cannot be said in a limited question and answer session in a seminar.

I hope this clarifies my view.
Rad Zdero

Letter #5
This letter was also written on a public internet blog in response to a gentleman who left remarks about my book Nexus: The World House Church Movement Reader, in which I illustrate and explain the difference between small groups, cell groups, and house churches. He was a cell church planter who felt I did not characterize cell churches accurately and that most house churches he knew were inward-looking and isolationist by choice. I wanted to briefly clarify my views and respond to a few specific points.

Hi Brother,

Thanks for your comment on the diagram and the description in my book. A few brief responses from me.

First, you are correct that some house churches are islands and do not wish to work with others. But the same can also be said of some cell churches and some traditional churches. In my book, I am not encouraging of those types of groups and, in fact, critique them.

Second, my diagram is meant to broadly represent various stages along a spectrum, knowing that there is certainly overlap between the three models. It is meant to oversimplify the analysis for the sake of discussion, not to be a definitive description that describes every possible variation.

Third, cell churches as very commonly practiced still do not fully allow each of the cells to function with full autonomy and there is always someone at the top of a leadership pyramid that needs to be consulted or followed. Any self-described "cell churches" that do give their "cells" full autonomy and yet work together cohesively, are functioning like the house church networks I describe. And I encourage that. In this case, it is a matter of semantics.

Thanks for your comments. And may the Lord multiply your life and ministry.

Rad Zdero

7

LETTERS TO DENOMINATIONS AND MINISTRIES

Letter #1

This letter was sent to the international director of a denomination which is supportive of small groups, as well as cell church and house church planting. He and I briefly exchanged emails about the concept of tithing and whether it is just an Old Testament practice or whether it is applicable to the church age. He sent me a booklet he wrote in support of mandatory tithing. This letter is my response to that booklet.

Dear Brother,

I hope you are doing well. Thanks again for sending along your booklet on why you believe mandatory 10% tithing is a legitimate practice for the church today. I recently read it and enjoyed it. As you already know, many in the house church movement, including myself, do not agree with this view. Instead, we believe compulsory 10% tithing is an Old Testament practice and that voluntary generous giving to God's work in the world is the New Testament way. I am not interested in a lengthy debate on this matter, since I don't think it will prove useful. But, I did want to offer some pros and cons about your booklet that may be helpful and also briefly explain the views and practices of many house churches I work with. I respect you despite our different views. And I welcome any response you care to give.

First, I liked several things about your booklet. You tried to ground everything you wrote on Scripture. The manuscript was logically organized. It was easy to read and not too technical, making it accessible to a wide audience. The tone was conciliatory and positive, while you did not shy away from communicating bluntly and passionately at times. There were several anecdotal stories which were helpful in understanding your view. Some practical examples were given that brought things from the realm of theory into the realm of reality. And you are obviously a man who is trying to consistently apply his convictions, as you illustrated from your own life a few times. Those were all good aspects of the booklet.

Second, your main focus in the booklet is a mandatory 10% tithe for Christians because you believe it is a legitimate carry-over from the Old Testament into the church. Yet, there is no mention that the Mosaic Law's tithes actually amounted to 23.3% of a person's annual income and belongings to support the Levitical priesthood, the festivals, and the poor (Lev 27:30-34; Num 18:21-31; Deut 14:22-29, 26:12-16; Mal 3:8-12). I think there is a need to be consistent within your own framework. My question is, what principle(s) of biblical interpretation promotes only 10% tithing as a mandatory church practice for Christians, rather than 23.3% tithing as actually taught in the Bible?

Third, you refer to Gen 14:18-20 where Abram gave 10% of his goods to Melchizedek and argue this principle should be applied by Christians, since the incident took place even before the Mosaic Law instituted the practice of 10% tithing. But, there are several things I'd like to point out. (1) There is, in fact, a direct link between Abram's act and regular mandatory tithing to support Levitical priests under the Mosaic Law (Heb 7:4-5,9); yet, this has been done away with through Christ, since "when the priesthood is changed, of necessity there takes place a change of law also" (Heb 7:12 NASB). (2) The record shows this was a one-time voluntary gift by Abram to Melchizedek, as far as we know. We cannot take a one-time voluntary event and turn it into a universal mandatory practice for the church. (3) The goods from which Abram tithed were obtained by his violent raid and defeat of an enemy king in order to recover stolen possessions. Certainly, I don't believe you would suggest Christians should physically conquer their enemies and then give a 10% tithe from their spoils of war. My question is, why do you apply to the church only one aspect of this passage (i.e. the 10% portion), but not the others, such as frequency (i.e. it was a one-time event), attitude (i.e. it was spontaneous, voluntary, and not commanded by God), and context (i.e. the goods given were from the spoils of war)?

Fourth, you make a brief mention of Abel giving the firstlings of his flock to the Lord (Gen 4:4) as possibly an example that influenced Abram when he gave 10% to Melchizedek. You qualify this statement by using the phrase "he may have learned this principle." I agree this is a possibility. But, without any clear evidence, this is just guesswork on anyone's part to link these two acts of giving. We have to be careful when making such statements to try to support a thesis when there is no evidence. Even so, the passage about Abel does not say he regularly gave a mandatory 10% tithe, but this also appears to be a one-time voluntary spontaneous act of giving to the Lord. Nonetheless, it is an example of a giving and generous attitude that we can all emulate.

Fifth, you refer to Malachi 3 to say that Old Testament believers were required to tithe so that the "storehouse" would be full. You then draw a parallel between the Old Testament "storehouse" and the New Testament local church to argue that Christians must give a 10% tithe to their local church. Although I don't believe in mandatory 10% tithing, I do agree with you that people should voluntarily financially support the work of their own local church. My issue here with your booklet is that there is an unclear use of Scripture in comparing the "storehouse" to the local church. There may be a more accurate scriptural parallel. Paul specifically compares the Temple service of Levites to the ministry of apostles (1 Cor 9:1,14-15), since Levites gave spiritual service to the entire nation of Israel while apostles give spiritual service to multiple churches. But, on a local level, first-century Jewish leaders of a local synagogue (i.e. rabbis) had their own jobs to support themselves and were not paid for their ministries (R.C.H. Lenski, *The Interpretation of St. Paul's Epistles to the Thessalonians, to Titus, and to Philemon*, 1946, p.683), which parallels what Paul says about local church leaders needing to support themselves (Acts 20:33-35). So, if anything, filling the "storehouse" of Malachi 3 may be a better parallel to financially supporting apostolic workers, rather than local church leaders.

Sixth, you quote a certain Christian leader who said that a principle of biblical interpretation is that whatever was established in the Old Testament remains applicable to the church unless the New Testament explicitly does away with it. Then you go on to write that mandatory tithing was an Old Testament practice that was never done away with explicitly in the New Testament and, therefore, it is binding on all Christians. In general, this is perhaps an acceptable "rule of thumb", but it may be problematic to apply this consistently and logically. It may be more accurate to say the Old Testament moral laws are to be carried over into the church age, but the ritualistic laws have been done away with in Christ (Gal 2:16-17; Heb 7:12). In any case, this is a tricky one, since there were many practices established in the Old Testament, both pre- and post-Mosaic Law, which were never explicitly disestablished in the New Testament. Yet, we do not continue to do them in the church. For example, stoning someone to death for Sabbath-breaking, forgiving all debts and releasing all prisoners every fiftieth year in the year of Jubilee, the Mosaic Law's practice of 23.3% tithing rather than just 10% tithing, etc. My question is, what principle(s) of biblical interpretation determines which Old Testament laws should be carried into the church and which should be stopped?

Seventh, you refer to 1 Cor 16:2 to argue Christians should give 10% tithes systematically and 2 Cor 9:7 to argue Christians should give 10% tithes and offerings gladly. There is a problem here with taking verses out of context. The record shows these passages specifically refer to an emergency fundraising campaign the apostles organized among the Gentile churches to help Jewish believers in Jerusalem suffering because of a famine in the time of the Roman emperor Claudius. The passages that give us the complete information on this particular situation are Acts 11:27-30, 1 Cor 16:1-3, 2 Cor 9:1-15, and Gal 2:10. These passages talk about a voluntary emergency one-time gift and cannot properly be used to promote mandatory systematic 10% tithing for the church.

Eighth, you refer to 1 Tim 5:17-18 to make the point that local church leaders (i.e. elders) should be funded through mandatory 10% tithing, since the word "honor" means giving financially. Certainly, it is tempting to believe so, since Paul also says here that the laborer deserves his wages and we should not muzzle an ox while it is threshing. However, I would like to challenge this view of 1 Tim 5:17-18. (1) The word for "honor" (Greek = *time*) is used over 40 times in the New Testament, meaning respect or value, but not finances. The Greek word for pay, wages, or salary (Greek = *misthos*) is used 38 times in the New Testament, but is not present in the phrase "double honor." (2) While visiting these same local elders in Ephesus on another occasion, Paul instructed them to financially support themselves and others (Acts 20:33-35). It would be a major contradiction if Paul suggested the church should pay elders on one occasion and then on another to say they should be financially self-supporting. (3) In the first-century Jewish synagogues—as precursors to the early Christian house churches—the spiritual elders/leaders were unpaid volunteers (R.C.H. Lenski, *The Interpretation of St. Paul's Epistles to the Thessalonians, to Titus, and to Philemon*, 1946, p.683). This surely influenced Paul in organizing house churches. (4) There was no practical reason for early house churches to pay local elders. A small team of four or five unpaid elders could easily have facilitated a house church, which usually had no more than 35 people (Del Birkey, *The House Church*, 1988, p.55).

Ninth, I am not interested in either rebelling against or upholding the institutional church's practices with respect to tithing. I am keen on what the Scripture says. And I want to allow the Spirit to guide me to address on-the-ground realities in the house church movement. What do I see in the Bible? Mandatory tithing is certainly practiced in the Old Testament by Jews (Mal

3:8) and is taught to Jews by Jesus prior to the church age (Matt 23:23), which began just after the Crucifixion-Resurrection-Pentecost event. But, there is not even a hint of mandatory tithing for Christians living in the church age. So, how did New Testament believers use their funds and resources? In essence, local leaders were interchangeably called elders/presbyters, pastors/shepherds, or overseers/bishops (Acts 20:17,28; 1 Pet 5:1-3). They were not supported financially for their ministry, but used their own finances to help others in the church (Acts 20:33-35). There was no need to give them regular salaries because an unpaid team of multiple elders/leaders (Acts 14:23; Rom 16:3-5; James 5:14; 1 Tim 4:14) could easily lead a New Testament-era house church, which usually had no more than 35 people according to archaeological findings (Del Birkey, *The House Church*, 1988, p.55). However, it was fine if someone wanted to give a special gift to a local church leader (Gal 6:6). Money and resources voluntarily given in the house churches were used to help support the poor and suffering (Acts 2:44-45; Acts 11:29; 1 Cor 16:1-3), as well as apostles who travelled widely, started new churches, grouped them into networks, visited them on occasion, and moved on to repeat the process (Luke 10:1-9; 1 Cor 9:1-15; Philip 4:15-19; 3 John 1:5-8).

Tenth, so how does voluntary generous giving practically work in many parts of the house church movement today? Our scriptural conviction is that mandatory 10% tithing was only an Old Testament practice, which has been replaced by the superiority of voluntary generous giving in the New Testament. There is an encouragement to communicate needs and opportunities, to be generous in giving, and to support missional activities. Some house churches have a bank account, while others have a cookie jar or shoe box to collect voluntary gifts. Some house churches issue receipts for income tax purposes, while others have chosen to avoid government involvement by not having a charitable tax number. Some house churches spontaneously give as circumstances arise, while others use the money they have already collected systematically. The money is used to support the activities of the local house church, the house church network, and also other missionaries and mercy ministries. Local house church leaders are not paid. Apostolic workers who travel widely are sometimes supported, while many choose to be "tentmakers" by supporting themselves. As you know, this is how many exploding house church movements are working, like our Chinese and Indian friends who give finances to travelling evangelists and apostles for outward kingdom expansion, rather than local leaders or facilities.

Finally, thanks for considering my thoughts on tithing versus giving with respect to the emerging house church movement today. I hope this letter is taken in good faith, knowing that I respect you despite our differences. I welcome any response.

All the best,
Rad Zdero

Letter #2
I wrote this letter on behalf of my house church co-labourer and myself. It was sent to the same denominational leader as in Letter #1. That denomination started experimenting with house churches. We sent him a copy of a training manual we developed. He received it gratefully and even referenced it in his book on house churches.

Greetings Brother,

I hope this note finds you doing well during these summer months and that you're able to get some rest and rejuvenation time. With all the travelling you're doing, it's unlikely you remember meeting both of us on separate occasions. One of us you met in the USA several years back, and the other you met twice in Canada during your talks on the emerging house church networks hosted by one of your representatives and his bunch.

We are in the process of planting a house church network (HCN) in our area under our own organization called HouseChurch.Ca, in cooperation with our denomination. We desire to see many house churches and networks planted in the greater Toronto area over the next 10 years.

We are aware that you are in the process of writing your book on HCNs and so have enclosed for your reference a copy of a leadership training manual we have developed, entitled *Save the World...Plant a House Church*. We thought you might be interested in some details on how a couple of crazy guys in Canada are going about planting an HCN.

As you'll notice, much of the material we use, of course, can be easily transferable to a small group ministry or cell church context. However, we have illustrated our vision for an HCN and how it is distinct from the usual Cell/Small Group Ministry in Module 2 on pages 12-15. Specifically, page 15 illustrates our desire to see single-cell and multi-cell house churches networked together in three ways: (1) large group gatherings of all house churches perhaps monthly, (2) a few mobile 5-fold ministers that do a circuit visiting each house church, and (3) the house churches themselves visiting each other house-to-house.

Just so you know, we are in periodic contact with your ministry representative in Canada and are both encouraged by and interested in your church planting school being developed. All for now. Thanks for your time.

Breathe deep,
Rad Zdero

Letter #3
This letter was sent to a number of North American denominational pastors or directors of church planting outside of the denomination I was involved with at the time. The intention was to see what kind of opportunities and openness there might be to work with others in helping launch house church movements in various contexts. Only a few people responded to me.

Dear Pastor or Director of Church Planting,
I hope this letter finds you doing well in life and ministry. As someone concerned with church planting and church growth, you may be familiar with, possibly considering, or currently utilizing

the "house church model" as a parallel approach in expanding God's kingdom.

As such, I am pleased to provide you with a complimentary copy of a book I have recently authored entitled, *The Global House Church Movement*. It details one approach among many that is being used of the Lord to disciple the nations today. My hope is that it will offer you biblical, historical, and strategic insights as you step ahead in your work of training emerging Christian leaders. Additional copies may be purchased directly from the publisher William Carey Library, www.MissionBooks.org.

Our denomination supports many types of church planting efforts, including the development of house church networks. We wish others in the body of Christ like you to succeed in their efforts to do so as well.

If you have any questions or would like to talk further about the possibility of house church networks as a strategy that your denomination or mission organization could embrace, please don't hesitate to contact me at your earliest convenience.

Best regards,
Rad Zdero

Letter #4

This letter was sent to the presidents of several well-known North American evangelical ministries. Because they were in touch with the mainstream evangelical community, I wanted to encourage them to keep informing and preparing the Body of Christ for the changes that were happening in the church worldwide. Only a few people responded to me.

Dear Brother,

I hope you are well these days. My name is Rad Zdero. I am a house church planter living in Canada. I write to you because you and your team are an influential voice and are able to reach into the homes of believers and non-believers alike.

As you know, there are many voices that the Lord is using to announce that an apostolic and prophetic reformation of the church is in process in our day. The Lord has also been speaking to many on these matters in an increasing way in recent years, including those like myself, who are specifically involved in the global house church movement.

To this end, I enclose for your consideration a copy of my recent book (as editor) entitled *Nexus: The World House Church Movement Reader*, published by the well-known mission publisher William Carey Library, www.MissionBooks.org.

Far from being a reactionary or rebellious trend, the world house church movement is motivated by the missional aspect of God's heart for the nations.

There are apostolic teams forming across the nations whose specific focus is saturating entire regions with the gospel by planting simple/organic "house church networks". I believe the Spirit of God is doing this. The result is that about 300,000 house churches have been planted globally between 1998 and 2006 (and that number does not include China!).

May I say that I am not writing to you primarily to promote this new book, but rather to encourage you and your team to prepare God's people for the very basic structural changes in church life and mission that are exploding around the world and that are beginning to happen in North America. You have had several good pieces that you aired on your show about the emerging house church movement. Please continue to keep the Christian public informed so that the Body of Christ can be prepared for the possible harvest and persecution that may be ahead in the near future.

With kind regards,
Rad Zdero

Letter #5
This letter was sent to several key regional and national leaders of my denomination with the hope of opening up some of the possibilities of seeing a real church planting movement emerge. The

letter resulted in an important leadership gathering organized by the denomination to explore ways of officially embracing different methodologies for planting new congregations.

Hello Brothers,

I hope you are both well. As always, it's nice to see both of you. I am forwarding this note to some others on the denomination's national leadership team, as it may be of interest to them in their roles. I would like to express some ideas that I did not initially wish to communicate at our last city pastors' meeting, but was more and more compelled to do so as the day unfolded post meeting.

Like you, I am somewhat concerned about the way church planting is currently situated within our denomination and the resource challenges we face. At that pastors' meeting, we heard one pastor say that the real burden he is facing is the construction project his church is taking on. Another said the crying need right now is for resources and facilities. And, an hour was spent talking about various ways to raise more money to meet these needs as a denomination. During that time, as I alluded to one of you privately, I was reminded of the Jesuit monk played by Robert DeNiro in the movie "The Mission", in which he voluntarily ties a heavy load of scrap materials to his body which he then drags around as he climbs mountains and crosses swamps, all as a form of self-punishment. It seems to me, that we as a denomination are doing the same thing; we have a millstone tied around our necks that we would rather carry around than cut loose. One pastor at that meeting proposed a paradigm shift regarding seeking out volunteer lay teams and catalytic people to plant churches. To me, this is a good step in the right direction, but more could be suggested.

Is it possible that the current resource crunch is God's way of saying to us that an additional paradigm shift is in order, one that involves cutting loose the millstone of expensive facilities for local churches and new church plants? As such, and not simply because this is a hobby horse of mine, allow me to propose two specific items for the upcoming denominational general conference.

First, can one of the denomination's subcommittees give serious consideration to proposing a paradigm shift within the denomination toward strongly urging the use of existing and free infrastructure already in place, i.e. people's homes, especially for struggling congregations and new church plants? These house church networks may be a solution to the resource challenge while still focusing on becoming a church planting movement. This may be a temporary financial stop-gap for many, while others may wish to continue on with the household model long-term.

Second, there is already a denominational subcommittee that deals with doctrine, but I would propose initiating one that focuses on church structure and polity in light of our resource challenge and the desire to become a church planting movement. In addition to the example of the early church, we have a wonderful heritage to draw upon regarding the effective strategy of the early Wesleyan movement of home-based "classes" and "bands". As a denomination, we are undergoing the transitional birth pangs of shifting from a congregational mentality to a movement mentality. We cannot maintain current church structures and patterns and the resources that go with it, while effectively engaging the growth opportunities we are encountering. As such, I believe it is vital for us to revisit the early church, the Wesleys, and what is happening around the world regarding church planting movements. Perhaps you can add this as an addendum to the minutes of the next pastors' meeting. Thanks for your consideration,
Rad Zdero

Letter #6
This letter was sent to pastors and church planters in my denomination to invite them to a conference, in which I was the keynote speaker, on house church planting in their area. I was working in partnership with a church planter from another denomination to organize the gathering. Several of these pastors and leaders attended, along with some Catholic priests, evangelical pastors, and numerous non-denominational believers.

Dear Pastor or Church Planter,
 I hope this note finds you doing well, in body and soul. I would like to invite you to an upcoming conference on planting house church networks that will be held in your region. The conference will be in both French and English languages.
 This may be of interest to you as you seek to reach your region for Christ. The conference may equip you with a new way of planting simple, inexpensive, participatory, and evangelistic house churches. Or, it may give you ideas about how to develop a strong cell group ministry in your current congregation.

Best regards,
Rad Zdero

Letter #7
This letter was sent to a pastor in my denomination who had an interest in a particular Latin American country. Some of my friends had visited some of this nation's house congregations connected with the denomination. My hope was that we could further supplement the development of these groups with the material I had developed. The project, unfortunately, did not materialize since this pastor advised me that the nation's Christian leaders would not embrace house churches as anything other than a default scenario due to their poverty and persecution.

Dear Brother,
 I hope this note finds you well in all areas of life and ministry. As for me, perhaps you have heard that I am struggling with significant illness, but many are praying and very supportive. God is using this time to speak to me about a number of issues.
 One of the things that I feel God has charged me with is to undergird efforts within the Body of Christ that are changing church structures that lead to more biblical and, hence, more effective church life and mission. During some recent prayer and reflection, an idea started to formulate regarding the emerging

house churches in this Latin American nation. Whether God's idea or mine, I am uncertain.

Would you spend some prayer time about the following? The idea would be to translate into Spanish either my entire book *The Global House Church Movement* or the "Biblical Foundations" chapter into a smaller booklet. This would be a limited printing of perhaps 100 to 200 copies to be freely distributed to key house church leaders. I hold all non-English translation rights as agreed with the publisher, so it would all be legal. It would be financed by interested folks. Distribution is something I am unsure of at this point.

My question to you is, would such a resource be wanted or needed there? Is there someone you know who is willing and able to carry out the translation? Would you be interested in involvement in this project? Do you see any potential for this outside that nation to help with other Spanish speaking simple church movements?

I will forward a copy of this letter to a good friend who also has a long standing interest and involvement in that country. Thanks for any suggestions and guidance.

In Christ,
Rad Zdero

Letter #8

This letter was sent to the leaders of my denomination indicating that my co-labourer and I, after seven years of involvement, were resigning our ministry from the denomination. This denomination was very open and supportive in everything they did for me, for which I was grateful. And I had no personal conflicts with denominational leaders. Over time, however, my discomfort grew with some of the centralized aspects of typical denominational structures, my growing conviction from Scripture and church history about the value of fostering a very flexible network of churches, the non-denominational and trans-denominational nature of the emerging network of house churches with which I was working, and some things the Lord spoke to me personally in a dream about what he wanted to accomplish. The dream was confirmed to me several times through some unusual circumstances.

Dear Brother,

We hope you are well. We are writing as a follow-up to our conversation about the relationship of our house church ministry as a church plant with the denomination.

Firstly, we have appreciated a number of things about our involvement with the denomination, which has provided us (a) legitimacy as we have worked with Christians and non-Christians in our context, (b) an official framework to accommodate us as planters of house churches, (c) a platform at commissions and conferences for communicating the vision and mission that God has given us, (d) partial financial support in the early stages of our mission, (e) training opportunities and resources, and (f) personal friendships.

Secondly, we have tried to contribute in some small way to helping shape and develop how the denomination engages in mission across the nation and beyond. We hope we have also been personally supportive of colleagues and friends in this context.

Thirdly, given your task as the director of church growth and development to develop official partnerships with church plants and planters, the need to clarify the relationship of our ministry with the denomination, and the apparently divergent path that our mission is taking us, it no longer seems appropriate or best that we continue on as an official church plant of the denomination. As such, with no hard feelings at all, we are formally withdrawing as a denominational church plant of the denomination.

Fourthly, we both expect and gladly welcome the fact that our paths in the future will cross yours and the denomination's as we both seek to follow Christ in planting churches to reach every person with the message of God's hope.

With respect and affection,
Rad Zdero

Letter #9

This is my personal resignation letter to the director of church growth and planting of my former denomination. It was written and sent at the same time as Letter #8. The director and I had a good and friendly conversation about the status of my house church ministry within the denomination and whether I wanted to keep working with them. It was this chat that made me realize it was definitely time to clarify matters for everyone concerned and then to move on in the direction God was calling me.

Dear Brother,

I hope you are well. I am writing as a follow-up to our conversation about my personal relationship as a church planter with, and as a member of, the denomination and the denomination's desire for some clarity.

I have expressed my thoughts and feelings about my connection with the denomination in the joint letter with my co-labourer and do not need to repeat them here in detail.

Put briefly, though, I feel I have benefited in numerous ways from the openness of the denomination in supporting me in this church planting effort. I will always appreciate this. I also hope that I have been supportive of friends and colleagues as they have stepped forward to plant new churches.

However, it seems apparent that our paths are diverging in the wood and, as such, it no longer seems appropriate for me to remain an official church planter or member of the denomination. Therefore, please consider this letter to be my formal resignation from the denomination.

With appreciation and affection,
Rad Zdero

8

LETTERS TO ELDERS OF HOUSE CHURCHES

Letter #1

This letter and Letter #2 were written to an elder of a house church who was concerned about some leadership meetings I helped establish among a network of house churches in my region. His contention was that no church meetings should ever be private or for leaders only, but rather they should be open to all in order to avoid potential elitism and the development of hierarchy among the house churches. We knew each other face-to-face and got along personally, although our friendship was relatively new.

Hello Brother,
    Thanks so much for your letter and the poem you sent along. It is much appreciated. The poem I actually shared with our house church at our last meeting, as we were talking about God's desire to mould us into useful vessels. Let me also add that I have thoroughly enjoyed our interactions and conversations and hope that we can continue connecting with one another. I thought it best also to respond in writing, as we are both very mobile individuals, and it is sometimes difficult to make a telephone connection. I would

like now to respond to your letter regarding the leadership issues you raised and some related comments.

I appreciate your candid comments and your willingness to act on what your convictions are, rather than convenience, as you put it. That is great! I would like to continue dialoguing with you on these issues with the hope of some resolution, since I can envision the benefits of partnering with one another and with other house churches to see some unity, cohesiveness, and cross-pollination as the Lord moves across this region. Iron sharpens iron!

One thing I am concerned about in this so-called "simple church" or "house church" movement is the possibility of it becoming merely a reaction to the traditional church and its sometimes very glaring flaws. My passion is to see house churches base their form and function, orthodoxy and orthopraxy, on Scripture. Sometimes this might overlap with traditional church practices, and other times it will look very different. Would you agree that if there is a clear New Testament practice, that we are to follow it for the health of the church? I am assuming that you will say yes.

With this in mind, I would like you to consider the following scriptural examples of elders/leaders meetings in the New Testament that were held apart from the rest of the body for the sake of focus. But, I agree, this is not to be motivated by convenience or practicality.

Paul and the Ephesian elders had a private meeting (Acts 20:17-38). Here Paul travels towards the city of Ephesus where the church has been established and organizes a private meeting only for the elders of the church. The record states that, "And from Miletus he sent to Ephesus and called to him the elders of the church. And when they had come to him, he said to them..." (Acts 20:17-18 NASB). Paul then proceeded to discuss with these elders various leadership issues like character, guarding the flock, working hard, etc., after which he commends them to God. Then they prayed. The Scripture is very clear that this was a private meeting for elders only, so they could address leadership concerns.

Paul and the Jerusalem church's leaders had a private meeting (Acts 15:2,6,23, 16:24; Gal 2:2). Here Paul and a few other apostles visit Jerusalem to have a meeting with those in leadership only, not with the entire church there. The Scripture states that, "And it was because of a revelation that I went up and I submitted to them the gospel which I preached among the Gentiles, but I did so in private to those who were of reputation." (Gal 2:2 NASB). The other Scriptures above bear out the fact that it was a leadership meeting of apostles and elders, although the rest of the church obviously knew about it.

Timothy trained a few faithful men (2 Tim 2:2). In this instance, Paul encourages Timothy—a young apostle—to focus particularly on a few potential leaders within the church to pass on the core of the gospel. Paul wrote to him, saying, "And the things which you have heard from me in the presence of many witnesses, these entrust to faithful men, who will be able to teach others also." (2 Tim 2:2 NASB). How is this to be done adequately apart from meetings with potential leaders, sometimes privately in order to focus on what needs to be discussed and prayed about? It is my contention that these faithful men were, in fact, the elders-in-training in the church there.

Jesus had an inner circle of 12 and also of 3 disciples. The Lord himself gave us an example here about investing in future generations of leaders by choosing 12 to be with him apart from the many followers he was gaining (Mark 3:13-14). Moreover, he then on occasion took Peter, John, and James alone to have private meetings with them, so they could be taught more deeply and be exposed to deeper experiences apart from the rest of the group (Mark 5:37, 9:2, 14:33).

Given these very clear scriptural examples of leadership meetings composed of apostles and elders, it seems to me that there is safety and precedent in pursuing my course of action in this emerging house church movement. To follow this biblical pattern will help adequately train, focus, and connect traveling and local leaders in future generations. And so, this is why we have elders meetings, not because of practicality and convenience only, but because there is biblical precedent and principle involved.

Thank you brother for taking the time to read my understanding of the Scriptures. I am open to further discussion and fellowship with you, as well as correction if I am not interpreting the

Scriptures clearly. Again, I hope we can figure out a way to partner together with one another in this Kingdom effort.

Thanks brother and peace of Christ,
Rad Zdero

Letter #2
The following letter I wrote to the same elder as in Letter #1, in order to continue our discussion on the whole issue of leadership meetings in the house church movement and other related topics. Our disagreement seemed to center on what the Scriptures actually taught, although we both agreed that we should allow the Scriptures to guide our understanding and practice.

Hello Brother,
    Thanks for your recent letter and your willingness to engage in dialogue around the issues at hand. I do hope this letter finds you doing well in all areas. I also appreciate the generous tone with which you wrote your last letter and hope that all our interactions—in agreement and disagreement—are of a high calibre in this regard. I will address and respond to your last letter in order.
    Regarding new wine and wineskins, you raise an excellent point concerning the apparent lack of "power" you have witnessed among many in the house church movement. Yes, to drink old wine even from new wineskins is to miss the point entirely. I agree. I would ask you to consider several questions though. Can one really discern from one or two visits with a church, or from limited interactions, the true spiritual state of that church? What does living in the power of the new wine really look like? Is it really definable? Is there not a danger of presuming to know whether such-and-such a church or individual is Spirit-led, without seeing the bigger picture of their lives or without having tracked with them for an extended period of time? My concern would be not to judge or evaluate too quickly a work—individually or corporately—that is ongoing and always in progress (Philip 1:6; James 1:4).

Allow me to give just a little clarification regarding our practice of having elders (i.e. leaders) meetings every month for the network of house churches. The main purpose is more for training and support, rather than dealing with internal church business of the individual house churches. We have found it immensely beneficial, encouraging, and instructive. This elders huddle is not truly "closed" in the sense that only those overseeing house churches can participate. There are a few folks who participate consistently and enthusiastically who do not currently oversee a house church, but they may indeed do so in the future. Anyone can join in, but there is an expectation of consistency and enthusiasm for all involved. But, it is mainly meant for current and potential elders and church planters. I hope this clarifies any miscommunication that I have given regarding our practice.

Concerning Paul and the Ephesian elders meeting (Acts 20:17-38), I agree with your point that context is very key in understanding the purpose of sayings and deeds in Scripture. What the proper and permissible application of that understanding is, is another issue altogether. Perhaps you feel that one-time events (e.g. Paul and the Ephesian elders meeting) should never serve to become normative practice for the church. But, this just begs a whole series of other questions. Is it permissible and profitable for the church to turn one-time events into a pattern? If not, why were these events recorded at all, if not for our instruction? Where does Scripture indicate that this should never be done? Even when an event is reported only once, does this imply that a similar type of event also never took place before or after? Did this meeting only take place once, or was it recorded only once to give us a glimpse of a routine that Paul had when he visited the Ephesian church and perhaps other churches too? Although you are correct that Paul taught publicly and from house to house, does not this private meeting with the Ephesian elders suggest that he may have done this on previous occasions? We will never know 100% the truth of the matter. But, let us assume that, as you suggest, that this was the only time Paul met with these elders privately. Allow me then to suggest that the fact that Paul would do this even just once, speaks to the permissibility and profitability of this as a pattern for the church. Why? In order to deal with church business, training, or for other reasons. I would not want to accuse Paul of bringing in a clergy/laity divide simply because he met with the elders privately, regardless of whether the purpose was for church business or personal encouragement or to say farewell.

Moreover, you make a distinction between church business, training of elders, and personal encouragement with respect to Paul's purpose in calling only the elders to meet with him. This is, I think, a valid distinction to some degree. Might I suggest, though, that there is much overlap and blurring of the lines among all three categories? How does one separate these issues properly? For example, training elders will also involve matters of the heart as much as matters of the hands and the head. As such, this meeting, far from being simply a personal one for Paul, also involved encouraging the elders themselves on a number of issues (i.e. training), so that they could properly oversee the church (i.e. church business). The content of Paul's message on this occasion was one of giving the elders a boost and further instructing them, in addition to his own benefit.

Also, if indeed this meeting was only for Paul's personal refreshment, as you contend, then why did he call only the elders together? Did Paul not have close ties with others in the church? Did he not know that this action might be construed as elitist? The fact that Paul called only the elders together suggests he had a particularly strong bond with them that he did not share with the rest of the church. How could this bond have developed? It was probably because he spent private time with them previously when he lived in Ephesus, since they were the elders and new elders-in-training that were overseeing the church.

With regard to the apostles stationed in Jerusalem, I would be interested in your understanding of the apparent clique or cloister of the 12 apostles in that city even after Pentecost. They seemed intent on maintaining a group of 12 at the centre of church life by choosing a replacement for Judas Iscariot (Acts 1:21-26). And they spent much time together in prayer and deliberation privately as a group (Acts 6:2-4). Does not this local apostolic core group act as a prototype for a local elders team? My question to you, then, would be whether you consider it improper for elders in a given city or town to ever meet for mutual support? Do you see this as an inappropriate activity? Did the New Testament elders from different house churches ever meet together for such support, planning, training, etc.? Does not the fact that various elders and house churches knew each other and were greeted by name in the same letters testify to the unity and cross-pollination that occurred locally (Acts 20:17; Rom 16; 1 Cor 16)?

Let's move on to the topic of Jesus and his inner circle of the 12 and the 3. Your main point in your last letter, as I understand it, was that Jesus was not acting with the intention of establishing church practice for future generations. His choice of the 12 and his interactions with them were primarily for the benefit of reaching Israel's lost sheep. Allow me to ask several questions. How do we treat the Gospels, since they record pre-Pentecost events, now that we are very much post-Pentecost? Do we ignore them on all accounts, which could be the extreme application of your thesis? Which criteria would you suggest for determining applications of the Gospels for the church? Was not Jesus very much aware that his actions, including the training of the 12 and the 3, would by default and necessity be the prototype upon which his followers would build the church? Was that not the reason why he trained the 12 in the first place? If Jesus' actions and words are not normative for the church, then we are building on the wrong foundation. He is the chief cornerstone around which the church is to be built. It seems to me that we are on safe ground in emulating Jesus, as Paul and the other apostles did.

Regarding your concern about our decision to form a network of house churches, I recognize, as you point out so well, that human reason and divine wisdom do not necessarily coincide on many occasions. However, I am of the conviction that God has given us brains to use in order to consider the signs of the times. As such, I would like to get your feedback—or at least for you to consider—how one would deal with certain practical realities without the formation of a tight network of house churches. For example, social needs can be met in a network, such as singles looking for a marriage partner and kids looking for playmates.

Psychological needs can be met in a network, such as the need to know that we are part of something other than our own house church and to see the bigger picture of what God is doing. Elders can be encouraged and trained better as part of a network, since there is more moral support and accountability from peers who deal with similar issues that perhaps other members in the house church don't have to face. I believe these are all spiritual matters that God is concerned about, rather than carnal or fleshly. My long-time involvement with small groups, cell groups, and house churches—since about 1985—tells me that these and other practical matters are best addressed in a deliberate fashion as part of a network of house churches. Anything less than that can easily default to a presumption about what God will and won't do to meet these practical needs. I personally don't want to be found abandoning the church, and the people that God entrusts to my care as an elder, by an act of omission or presumption. Please don't misunderstand me here. I am not implying that you are doing that if you choose a different course of action on these matters.

Thank you brother for reading this letter and for your willingness to dialogue openly and respectfully. I appreciate your zeal for God and his people. My sense is that we have more we agree on than not and that this is a good starting place for future conversation and perhaps even collaboration.

Peace of Christ,
Rad Zdero

Letter #3
This letter was sent to an elder of a house church who believed only men were permitted to be leaders in the church, that women could only speak in church meetings to a limited degree, and that marriage and many children were God's ideal will for most people.

Hi Brother,
    I hope you are well and that your trip to the house church in the USA was fruitful. Again, you are missed when you are not

able to attend our network meetings. But, I respect your willingness to do what you feel is right in not attending, since we had a woman scheduled to teach at that time. Thanks for your very interesting email from the other day on "family unplanning". I read it and do agree with some of the remarks about the sometimes not-so-positive influence of cultural shifts on families, marriage, and children. These are some good points to be sure. And I appreciate the desire of the writer to be faithful (and yours) to what he believes the Lord is asking him and his family to do. I do have some concerns, though, that one does not judge too quickly those people who may not be married but are grown adults, or who are married and yet do not have any or many children. There are many Bible reasons and other factors that need to be considered, for both men and women, such as those below.

There were characters in the Bible who were single, never married as far as we know, and yet used mightily by God, such as the Lord Jesus, John the Baptist, Paul the apostle, Philip's four daughters who were prophetesses, Luke (early church documents tell us he never got married), prophets like Elijah, etc.

There is encouragement in the Bible that singleness is a superior lifestyle if one is able and called to it, such as that stated by the Lord Jesus (Matt 19:10-12) and by the apostle Paul (1 Cor 7:7-9,17,25-40). Paul specifically suggests this for both men and women.

There are examples in the Bible that God's timing for a person to get married, or to have children, may not be the same as what we think makes sense or what we would like. God's timing was very different and much longer for certain promises to be fulfilled than the people themselves perhaps expected. For example, Abraham and Sarah to have Isaac (25-year wait), David to become king (13-year wait), Paul to be sent as an apostle to the Gentiles (10-year wait), Joseph to become that leader over his family (13-year wait), Moses tended sheep for 40 years before being sent back to Egypt by God, etc. Sometimes, Bible people did not get married until very late, such as Isaac at 40 years old (Gen 25:20) and Esau at 40 years old (Gen 26:34). Thus, it is certainly possible that God desires that some be married and have children earlier, but that others remain single or get married much later in life, because of the other things that God may be calling them to do instead, such as ministry, mission, character development, education/training, and career/stability, or because it is not God's timing until some other things are set in place.

There were married couples in the Bible who had one or few children, such as Noah (3 children, namely Shem, Japheth, Ham, see Gen 7:13), Zacharias and Elizabeth (one child, namely John the Baptist, see Luke 1:6-13), Zorah and Manoah (one child, namely Samson, see Judges 13:2-5), Elkanah and Hannah (one child, namely Samuel the Prophet, see 1 Sam 1:2-11), Abraham and Sarah (one child, namely Isaac, see Gen 18:11-15, 21:1-3), Isaac and Rebekah (two children, namely Jacob and Esau, see Gen 25:21-26), Samuel the Prophet (two children, see 1 Sam 8:1-2), etc.

There are personal circumstances such as barrenness, mental problems, medical problems, financial instability, legal issues (e.g. China, where 1 to 2 children is the maximum allowed legally), also prevent many people from marriage or bearing children.

Regarding whether Rom 16:7 refers to a female apostle named "Junia" or a male apostle named "Junius", this entire area is of course debated among very sincere, godly, and scholarly teachers in the Church. There are many Scriptures that need to be brought to bear on the matter, not just one, as we briefly discussed on the telephone. It is not as clear cut as some suggest. Some books which I plan on reading that deal with all sides of the issue are Kostenberger and Schreiner, *Women in the Church*, Clouse and Clouse, *Women in Ministry: 4 Views*, and Mickelsen, *Women, Authority, and the Bible*. I appreciate the quote you sent, and it is worth considering. Yet we must also be careful since we can produce many quotes from scholars to support this or that view. Even so, here is another comment about who Junia was:

"It is possible to search the writings of the early church fathers who were much closer to the original manuscripts and church than we are today. John Chrysostom (337-407), bishop of Constantinople, wasn't partial to women. He said some negative things about women but spoke positively about Junia: 'Oh, how great is the devotion of this woman that she should be counted worthy of the appellation of apostle.' Nor was he the only church father that believed Junia was a woman. Origen of Alexandria (185-253) said the name was a variant of Julia (Rom 16:15), as does Thayer's Lexicon. Leonard Swidler cited Jerome (340-419), Hatto of Vercelli (924-961), Theophylak (1050-1108), and Peter Abelard (1079-1142) as believing Junia to be a woman. Dr. Swidler stated: 'To the best of my knowledge, no commentator on the text until Aegidus of Rome (1245-1316) took the name to be masculine.' Apparently the idea that Junia was a man's name is a relatively modern concept but the bulk of the best evidence available is that Junia was indeed a woman, and an outstanding apostle." (Charles Trombley, *Who Said Women Can't Teach?* 1985, pages 190-191).

Alright brother, I will end the email here. Perhaps this will be a topic that you and I will continue to discuss and explore and maybe disagree in the future, in light of Scripture, as "iron sharpens iron". But I am sure all will be done with mutual respect and a desire to seek truth. I look forward to your teaching next month. My best regards to your family.

In Christ,
Rad Zdero

Letter #4
This letter was sent to an elder (different from Letter #3) who responded to an article I wrote which argued that women in the New Testament functioned in all contexts and roles. He thought women could be apostles, since this involved evangelism of non-believers and speaking in a house church, but they should not be overseers of a house church nor should they speak when multiple house churches met.

Hi Brother,
　　Thanks for your email. And for your partnership in the gospel. The "women" article I wrote was meant to highlight some points

that people miss, not to get into a detailed discussion of everything related to the issue. So I was not able to explain every possible objection. Briefly, I would say just a few things to a couple of your comments.

I believe an "elder" (Greek = *presbuteros*) is, in fact, an "overseer" (Greek = *episkopos*) and a "shepherd" (Greek = *poimen*), since all three terms are used to address the same group of people in Acts 20:17,28 and 1 Pet 5:1-5. So, if a woman can be a house church elder, by definition she is actually an overseer/pastor.

If you agree that women can be apostles, how are they going to raise up a church if they are not allowed to speak and must be silent in certain gatherings? So, must a mature apostolic woman (say 20 years in the Lord) be silent while trying to train up spiritually immature or non-believing men who are just joining the new congregation or who just happen to walk into the room?

The young woman you talked with who said, "Rad is stretching it, since how can a woman be the husband of one wife?", I believe, is entirely missing the point. The connecting Greek word "likewise" connects the general characteristics of male elders and applies them to female elders in 1 Tim 3:11, not the literal details. If we take everything Paul says literally and mechanically, then single men like me (who are also not the husband of one wife) can never be overseers of a local church. And that does not make any sense at all.

The spiritually mature Christian women who led and/or hosted house churches in the New Testament, like Priscilla and Lydia and Chloe and Apphia, surely, were not just baking cookies, teaching children, and keeping silent, as soon as a man walked into the room, even if that man was only one day old in the Lord and knew nothing about the Bible.

Being mentioned first (e.g. Priscilla and then Aquila) is an important detail indicating prominence, because in the ancient Greek world this was the culturally common thing to do. And even your point about first Barnabas, and then Paul, being mentioned on some occasions agrees with this. Why? In one instance, the Greeks believed that the chief speaker Paul (being like the Greek messenger god Hermes) was simply representing Barnabas (being like the chief god Zeus) (Acts 14:11-12).

Anyway brother, that's all I wanted to say, without getting into a long drawn out discussion and detailed analysis. Thanks for your open mind and willingness to dialogue and co-labour together. Give my best to the family.

Best regards,
Rad Zdero

Letter #5
This letter was sent to an elder of a house church that I first met at one of our national conferences I helped organize. His main concern was that house churches not become groups that were merely reacting against the institutional church, but who were also motivated by opposing some of the big problems of the day like war, poverty, homelessness, government oppression, environmental degradation, and so forth.

Hi Friend,
　　Thanks for your input in your last email. I and some others in the house churches agree with you on some of these issues. See my "Christ and Caesar" article in the resources section of my website. Some of us have already begun talking about these matters.
　　Before we can deal with these deeper issues, we have to spend time together to build trusting relationships and deal with some basic issues of networking and mission and finances, and even then we will have some disagreements and "camps" emerging.
　　I envision that in time we will start dealing with these other deeper issues, but baby steps are needed first. We can't skip steps. That's the way I see it anyway.
　　What I could do is add these issues on to the list of issues I was planning to email to everyone to begin considering before the next national leaders meeting. At least that would start the dialogue at the national level.

But, maybe you can write an article on these issues for our *Starfish Files* magazine. Some version of your last email would suffice as an article perhaps. I guess I could write an editorial just to bring these issues up too.

Okay, all for now,
Rad Zdero

Letter #6
The following letter was written to the elders of a house church which was part of a fledgling network of groups I had helped start. Our network was just at the point of expanding enough that we felt it necessary to have some people circulate among the groups just to keep them encouraged. It gives a glimpse into an early stage in the ongoing process of pioneering a network of house churches.

Hi Friends,
 I hope your house church is well. Just a little something you should know. I write this to encourage you (and myself) and to keep you in the information loop.
 We have been making some connections with folks who currently have stand alone house churches and people who want to start groups, but want to be plugged into a tight network of house churches. We are thinking of restarting a new training huddle for these folks or inviting them to possibly join in with the current group.
 We have been talking about possibly introducing the idea of a "circuit rider" to visit individual house churches from time to time, maybe monthly or every other month. This would keep people encouraged and connected to the bigger picture and focused. Would this appeal to you? We are thinking this would be in addition to the monthly leadership huddles that we have for our network of house churches.
 It is very easy at this point in the process to lose heart and vision and focus, since there are so few of us doing this at the moment, and sometimes we wonder why. We are not yet at a critical mass

and we, especially people like me, need to learn the patience of the farmer, who sows the seed and needs to wait for a long time for the harvest to come. All for now. Let's keep connected.

All the best,
Rad Zdero

Letter #7

This short note was written to an elder of a house church who had some tension with the elder of another house church in their region over doctrinal issues. It was not a personality conflict, but purely theological. Although the issue was important, i.e. whether the Trinity is scriptural, it was not a matter of them doubting the other's salvation. Unfortunately, they could not bridge the gap.

Hi Brother,

Thanks for this warning. I'll respond just very briefly. Sure, I can take your name off the contact list. In my thinking, it would be good to keep it in case people wanted to plug into a house church in your area, but I will respect your wishes to have it removed (sigh).

I was aware that our mutual friend had some issues about the Trinity, but conceded to me that he could see that John 20:28 did indicate Jesus was indeed God in the Greek and that he was still open to the idea from Scripture. I will read through the web link that you gave me written by him and the various folks. Thanks.

About the article that our mutual friend wrote about using the Bible, I'm not sure what your objection might be. I do hope that your house church is making use of the Bible in your meetings. It's easy to go off the track without it. I hope your two apostolic advisors are not discouraging you from using the Bible, other than maybe for a short season to "detoxify" from your previous institutional church experience.

I sense great tension in your email. I'm sorry to hear about the damaged relationship between you and our mutual friend. I would encourage you and him to dialogue openly and honestly, and forgive where missteps were made on either side. Otherwise, that sort of bad feeling just festers and does injury to one's own self and ministry. "Forgive us our debts as we forgive others..." may be something to ponder.

All for now,
Rad Zdero

9

LETTER TO APOSTLES OF HOUSE CHURCHES

This letter was written to several people in different nations who had a clear apostolic role among the house churches. I had worked with a couple of them in the cause of Christ in various ways. One of them asked me to provide some mentorship on an ongoing basis. It was this request that challenged me to distil in writing what my understanding of the work of an apostle was in the context of the growing house church movement.

Dear Friend,

How are things with you? I hope the answer is "excellent." I'm writing to encourage you as you step ahead in your role of overseeing and catalyzing a network of missional house churches. I hope this letter adds to the dialogue we've already had. I write to you and a few other individuals in other nations. Because it may not be practical for me at this time to interact with you on a regular basis, I want to communicate to you my understanding of the essentials of the apostolic work you are involved in. I'd like to touch on just a few biblical and practical matters about the necessity for apostles in the house church movement and the responsibilities, qualifications, and risks. Whether you would use the word "apostle" for yourself is not really that important. What is vital is to recognize that this is the kind of work you are doing. Certainly, I don't pretend to have this all figured out myself, nor would I place myself in the position of being the man with all the answers. And this letter is by no means comprehensive. Nonetheless, I trust that some of my experiences and understanding may be of benefit to you. And so, with that stated, prayerfully consider the following.

We Need Apostles

There is a great need for genuine apostles to arise within the house church movement today. I don't mean that we should expect there to be primary-type apostles who lay down new doctrine and revelation, or who are in the same category as the Twelve or Paul. Rather, I mean that there have always been throughout church history—and there are today—secondary-type apostles who can carry out some pioneering, organizing, and overseeing functions like Apollos, Timothy, and Titus. How does this apply to the house churches today? Many groups meet in homes and other places and call themselves "biblical", "simple", "organic", "missional", or "house" churches. However, many have been prototyped incorrectly or unwisely. They may never reach their intended divine destiny because they are not linked to an apostle, but rather a prophet, evangelist, teacher, or pastor. Apostles, however, by their unique gifting from the Lord, are able to provide the vision, training, networking, team building, resourcing, and problem solving needed to bring missional, relational, devotional, and doctrinal health to the church with Jesus Christ as the chief cornerstone. Of course, apostles cannot do this on their own, but only as they work with and link together the prophets, evangelists, teachers, and pastors (Acts 8:14, 15:6, 20:17; Eph 4:11-12). For instance, in my country and region, I know a number of groups that would fall into one of these following categories. *Isolationist* groups want nothing to do with outsiders and wish to remain unto themselves for fear of getting sucked into a denomination. *Ingrown* groups are often too focused on the relationships with each other without any concern for the world out there. *Idolatrous* groups are personality cults because they look to their founding leader for all the answers. *Information-based* groups have a theological hobby horse and make Bible study their main thing. *Inspiration-based* groups focus on an emotional or spiritual experience as their reason for existence. *Impact-driven* groups are so outreach-minded that their sole focus is on growth, expansion, and numbers. All of these are unbalanced and, therefore, unhealthy house churches. Yet, as several of us brought together various leaders and groups over several years for a series of "think tanks" to build relationships, share stories, ask questions, pray, play, and eat, the interpersonal trust has been built, people's vision has been expanded, and the house churches have now started to work together and cross-pollinate their strengths and resources.

Apostles are Talkers

Talking until you are blue in the face is not always bad. Apostles are sent by God to either a people that has not heard the name of Christ or to an existing Christian community to strengthen them. An apostle who wants to remain utterly silent and stay in the background is no apostle at all, or at least, is not fulfilling one of their responsibilities. Apostles are meant to be out in the open, seen in a public context, and constantly either preaching to the unsaved or teaching the saved. There are many books, courses, and groups that can help an apostle sharpen their verbal skills. Practicing in private or in front of a trusted group of friends who will give you feedback on verbal strengths and weaknesses is valuable. Paul the apostle knew he was commissioned to preach and teach (Acts 15:35, 18:9, 20:20-21). He tried to verbally persuade Jews and Gentiles to come to faith in Jesus Christ (Acts 17:2,3,17,22). He taught fellow believers (2 Tim 2:2). He dialogued late into the night (Acts 20:7). He debated other Christian leaders (Acts 15:2,38-39; Gal 2:11-21). He sometimes needed to defend or explain his ministry (Acts 15:12, 21:19; Gal 2:2). Verbal skill, thus, is paramount for the apostle. A personal example may be helpful. I once organized a house church conference in which a small team of five were to come and interact and speak to 50 or so attendees. I was very focused on making sure the practical matters were handled well such as the facility, food, drinks, schedule, resources, etc. And during most of the sessions, I sat at the back of the room simply ensuring the event was running smoothly. I did not say much, other than to keep the event on schedule. A prophetic friend of mine then approached me and said to me, "God has not created you to be silent and to sit at the back of the room. Now is the time for you to step forward into the public eye." I took that to heart. Others have said similar things. Although I've never had any fear of public speaking, I never wanted people to think I was trying to attract attention to myself. Since I have increasingly begun to speak publicly as I felt God lead, people have affirmed my message and my competence in this area.

Apostles are Writers

The pen is mightier than the sword. World history has shown how spiritual, political, and cultural movements have been spawned or supported through the written word. The apostolic letters of the New Testament helped establish the message of Christ in the early days of the church (Luke 1:1-4; John 20:31; Acts 15:20,23; Rom 15:15; 2 John 1:12; 3 John 1:9). The writings of John Wycliffe, Martin Luther, John Calvin, George Fox, John Wesley, and others brought cohesion to various reform, renewal, and revival movements within Christianity. The novels of Tolstoy, Dostoyevsky, and Dickens have inspired generations to strive for the nobler aspects of humanity. The literature produced by Marx, Lenin, and Mao spread the ideology of communism around the globe. For good or ill, books, pamphlets, letters, magazines, charters, and so on, can powerfully articulate the principles and practices of an idea. In my view, an apostle who speaks but does not write, is like a boxer trying to fight with one hand tied behind his back. An apostle must hone his or her writing skills to inform, instruct, involve, and inspire. We know more about the apostle Paul the man, as well as his message and ministry, precisely because he put things down in writing, more so than the other apostles. Remember, half the New Testament books were written by Paul. So, do whatever it takes to get better at it. Take a creative writing class. Study the writing styles of those who have influenced you. Commit to writing a little bit every day in your diary or journal. Ask trusted friends to evaluate and edit what you write.

And, of course, apostles have to be keen learners themselves, if they are to help others. So, make sure you read widely and start building your own personal library of books, videos, CDs, and other resources. In my own case, many people over the years have said very complimentary things. And there has been a prophetic word or two on the matter. And so I have been encouraged in my efforts. The Lord has opened the door to see a number of my works published, such as poems, short stories, scientific articles in academic journals, textbook chapters, a novel, and two books on the house church movement, as well as editing a house church magazine with an international readership. Some have been translated into other languages. The point is that God's gift through anyone can touch many people that they might otherwise never come into contact with.

Apostles are Travelers
Hit the road! This is the refrain that every apostolic worker needs to memorize. An apostle needs to interact face-to-face with the house churches and leaders they serve. In our modern age, we have conveniences like telephones, emails, faxes, television, and other technologies that cut down the distance between people. But, I believe that nothing quite compares to personal human interaction in building relationships and imparting truth. A stationary apostle is a contradiction in terms. Of course, apostles may have a city or region as their scope of ministry from the Lord, like James in Israel (Acts 15:1 compare with Gal 2:12) and John in Asia Minor (Rev 2 and 3; compare with 2 John 1:12 and 3 John 1:14). Some may be called to a particular people group, like Peter, James, and John to the Jews (Gal 2:9). Others may be called to an international work, like Paul and Barnabas (Gal 2:9). Whatever the case, apostles have wheels on their feet (Acts 15:36). I personally know apostles within the simple, organic, house church movement who fall into each of these categories. And sometimes God will extend the scope of an apostle's influence depending on the need and their readiness. One married couple I know, for example, started a few house churches in their city. Then they helped link several networks in their region. Then they became

involved in influencing their nation through a national publication and conference. Now they are traveling widely from nation to nation, visiting and encouraging house church networks and leaders wherever they go. In my own case, I have travelled extensively in my own region to resource, train, encourage, and simply spend time with leaders and house churches in one-to-one, small group, and conference settings. One particular trip involved 2200 kilometres of driving to visit 7 cities over a period of 2 weeks in one continuous circuit. Despite my fear of my motivations being misunderstood, everywhere I went people welcomed me with open arms and were thankful to know they were not alone and that someone cared enough to visit them. It was exhausting, but eye opening. I was grateful to the Lord for giving me the privilege of seeing things that many never have the chance to see.

Apostles are Pioneers
Pioneers are the first ones to see the possibility of a new idea becoming a reality. They are usually ignored at first. Then they are mocked. And then they may be attacked or opposed. Some will die or quit. But, just as often, many will succeed in giving birth to their dream. Anyone who has started a business, club, organization, or other project, knows how much time and energy and motivation are needed. Only true pioneers are willing and able to tackle the challenge of starting something from nothing. More traditional missionaries and church planters often have a hard time starting a new ministry using widely accepted and recognized forms and approaches. How much more difficult is this task for those in the house church movement, especially in nations where an institutional model of the church has a long history? So, like Paul, pioneers among the house churches must take initiative (Acts 15:36), be patient (Gal 6:9), endure resistance (2 Cor 11:23-28), and envision the future (2 Cor 10:14-16). What is it that an apostle will pioneer? They will start new churches, foster new disciples, train new leaders, establish new networks, and then move on to new territory to repeat the process. The key word here is "new." By way of illustration, most of today's church planting movements of the Southern Baptists outside North America are house church

movements. Missionaries, who are really functioning like apostles, will go into an area, reach a few new people with the gospel, or begin to work with a small group of Christians. They help them plant some new house churches. Then they train the new disciples and turn them into new leaders who become captivated by the vision of reaching their people group with the gospel. These new believers and leaders will go from door to door and village to village to see new house churches planted. Soon enough, they have a multiplying movement on their hands, with the original missionary becoming less and less involved. Once a healthy and growing network of house churches has been established, the missionary leaves to begin the same process elsewhere. This has been called the MAWL approach, i.e. Model, Assist, Watch, and Leave. These letters should be tattooed on every apostle's brain.

Apostles are Problem Solvers
You don't have to go looking for trouble. It'll find you. Especially if you are an apostle. Problems can come from the Enemy, the church, or the self. The Enemy's strategy is to use governments, economies, and cultures to block apostles from traveling, speaking, and writing. The church brings conflict the apostle's way through doctrinal, moral, and personal conflict. And, ironically, apostles themselves will have to face their own fears, weaknesses, and temptations, which may be greater barriers to bearing spiritual fruit than the other two sources. Whatever the case, the apostle's job is to keep true to their message and methodology, while decisively dealing with heresy, slander, divisiveness, persecution, temptation, and so forth. We see many similar situations in the early church and how the apostles had to become expert problem solvers for things to move forward. When heresy reared its ugly head from Jerusalem, of all places, the apostles and elders got together to debate and then decide about how to deal with the influx of Gentiles into the church (Acts 15:1-30). When indecision about where to extend their missionary travels became an issue, the Lord gave Paul a dream which helped the team decide that Macedonia was the place they needed to go (Acts 16:6-15). When imprisonment was threatened, the apostles decided their

best approach was to stand resolutely against their oppressors and continue to preach and teach about Christ (Acts 4:1-20,29). When famine struck the land of Judea, the apostles decided to start a fundraising campaign among the Gentile churches to raise money to help the Jewish believers in Christ (Acts 11:28-30; 2 Cor 9:1-15). Similarly, I know of a large nationwide network of house churches in a Southeast Asian nation which recently had a full-day national leadership meeting. I was sent a personal copy of the proceedings of the meeting by one of their main apostolic leaders. They made practical decisions about finances, allocated resources and people, assessed current strengths and weaknesses, re-evaluated their leadership structure, determined how to enhance their training materials, reviewed an update report on church growth, set dates for regional conferences, and so on. The document was peppered with people's names, which emphasized to me that the problem solving and decision making was undergirded by the personal relationships they had with one another.

Apostles are Builders

No man is an island, or so the saying goes. And the same is true for apostles. For apostles to accomplish what God has asked them to do, they will need to learn the art of building! They are, in the apostle Paul's words, wise master builders who lay the foundation of Jesus Christ and must constantly evaluate their work to see if it will withstand the pressures of reality (1 Cor 3:10-15). Specifically, they need to build three things in an ongoing process. They need to build up a local body of believers into a unit that functions corporately under the headship of Christ (Acts 20:17,20; 1 Cor 12:7-12,27-30; 1 Cor 14:26). They need to build a team of coworkers who can partner together to accomplish greater goals (Mark 3:13-14; Luke 10:1-11; Acts 20:4). They need to build partnerships with other apostolic leaders farther afield into a loose but functional network (Gal 2:9). If not, they will find themselves toiling all alone with few results that outlast them. A perfect example is the difference between George Whitefield and John Wesley, the famous catalyzers who worked together for a season to usher in the First Great Awakening in 18th-century Britain and

America. Whitefield, a far better speaker than Wesley, proceeded to travel extensively and use his great oratory skills to see many people come to Christ, whom he then encouraged to join the existing churches of the day. Wesley, however, would not preach anywhere unless he was permitted to follow-up with new converts and organize them into small home groups of "classes" and "bands" for discipleship and accountability, which were in turn plugged into a citywide, regional, and national network of leaders and groups. Near the end of his life, Whitefield said despondently that he had woven a rope of sand, since there was no visible fruit or movement he could identify resulting from his labours. At Wesley's death, however, his cohesive network included over 10,000 home groups with 100,000 believers in what became the Methodist movement. Whitefield blessed! But, Wesley built!

Apostles are Strategists

A picture is worth a thousand words, so the saying goes. But I like to say that a map is worth ten thousand! A vital role of an apostle is that of the strategist who sees the big picture, knows what needs to be done, is able to gather all the required resources, understands the enemy's tactics, and then gets the job done. He or she is just like a General mobilizing and leading an army to victory on the battlefield. God always has a specific plan, and an apostle's job is to receive that information from the Lord and implement it. The Lord Jesus had a plan and "appointed seventy others, and sent them two and two ahead of Him to every city and place where He Himself was going to come." (Luke 10:1 NASB). We also know that Paul went "from Jerusalem and round about as far as Illyricum I have fully preached the gospel of Christ. And thus I aspired to preach the gospel, not where Christ was already named, that I might not build upon another man's foundation." (Rom 15:20 NASB). At other times, Paul's plan was to "return and visit the brethren in every city in which we proclaimed the word of the Lord, and see how they are." (Acts 15:36 NASB). Here's a practical idea I could recommend, since I have done something similar and found it very helpful regarding encouraging and linking the house churches. You can get a big map of the geographic region you are called to impact with the gospel. Put a Scripture or a mission statement at the top of the map. Start praying, thinking, and planning. Put pins in the map showing the locations of existing house churches, leaders, evangelistic hot spots, or unreached areas. Circle areas where there is a clustering of house churches. Identify locations central to the house churches for future conferences or training points. Determine strongholds of the Enemy where immorality, false religion, persecution, materialism, and so on, are dominant and gather a team to tear down the strongholds through prayer. Another real-life illustration would be that of Dawson Trotman who founded the Navigators, a ministry that takes 2 Tim 2:2 to heart by focusing on friendship evangelism, one-to-one discipleship, and small groups. Dawson would pull out a map and pray every day for specific nations, believing God would establish a work in those countries. Today, the Navigators are located in over 100 nations and are one of the largest evangelical mission agencies in the world. To some people all this seems silly, presumptuous, or overly-planned. Of course, any plans or ideas must come from the Spirit and should not be implanted mechanically. But, as John Wesley once similarly said, let's get organized to beat the devil!

Apostles are Commissioned

A true apostle is never self-appointed. They don't wake up one morning and decide they want to be an apostle, read some books, take some courses, get a certificate, and then apply for the job. Rather, apostles are always commissioned by the Lord and recognized by a community of faith as having the character, competence, and calling of an apostle. Those who are false or immature apostles, driven by ego and others appetites, will eventually be detected by discerning believers (2 Cor 11:13; Rev 2:2). We are told that, after a night of prayer, Jesus chose 12 to be his disciples, so that he could train them to become apostles (Matt 10:1; Mark 3:13-14; Luke 6:13). Paul and Barnabas were selected by the Spirit to be sent out as apostles, as discerned by a group of leading teachers and prophets in Antioch (Acts 13:1-3). Timothy, a younger apostle trained and recruited by Paul (Acts 16:1-3; 1

Thess 1:1,2:6; 2 Tim 2:2), was launched into his ministry during the laying on of hands by a groups of elders (1 Tim 4:14). Now for some practical suggestions on recognizing genuine apostles. *Character* means they have a godly handle on time, money, sex, alcohol, ego, marriage, family, job, and so on, as well as displaying a deep passion for Christ. *Competence* means they have a proven track record of starting or leading a house church or house church network and/or they are already functioning at a high level as a prophet, evangelist, teacher, or elder/pastor. *Calling* means they have a clear personal sense of God asking them to step into this role and that this is confirmed by other believers, including those already functioning as apostles. There doesn't have to be any formal "ordination" ceremony, as often done in the institutional church, but it is probably a good thing to mark this milestone with a simple time of prayer and commissioning of the apostle even by a small body of believers. Often, apostles "grow into" their role by the suffering and toil and fruit of their ministry, long before they or others ever start to apply the term "apostle" to them. After all, it is the impact of the work of an apostle, not any public recognition or praise or title, that proves their genuineness (1 Cor 3:9-15, 9:1-2; 2 Cor 11:5,23-28). For example, I just received a ministry report today, as I was writing this, from an apostle in an Asian nation who has started 11,500 rural house churches in the past 9 years. Nowhere in the document do they ever use the word "apostle." Yet, he and his coworkers are doing apostolic work. They are not interested in titles, they are just interested in seeing people won, built, and sent into the harvest fields for Jesus Christ!

Well, there you have it. Pray about it, think about it, and act on it as the Spirit leads. Yes, more things could be said about apostles as mentors, networkers, encouragers, protectors, examples, and so forth. But, I hope these highlights will encourage you to pursue your calling to even more vigorously lead, mobilize, and multiply your swelling network of missional house groups. I welcome your response.

Pax Christi,
Rad Zdero

10

LETTERS TO NETWORKS OF HOUSE CHURCHES

Letter #1

The following letter was sent to the leadership team of a cohesive network of house churches that I helped start and with which I continued to be deeply involved. Written during a time of recovery from extended illness, it was my way of staying in touch with this leadership team. More importantly, I felt the Lord ask me to write it.

Dear Sisters and Brothers,

    I hope this note finds you prospering in body and spirit. I write specifically to you as a small cluster of house churches. I write as one brother to my fellow pilgrims on our joint venture of faith. I feel that I need to share some things with you that God has been asking me to write for about 10 days now.

    Let me initially say how much I am thankful that a number of you have been praying for my full recovery bodily (and in soul) during this time of illness and trial I am undergoing. The Spirit has been telling me many things these past 5 to 6 weeks. I won't share them here. I have been praying for you also. So, thanks very much to you all who are supporting me in this way.

But, now to the real point of this letter. At the last meeting of the elders/leaders of the house churches, which I was unable to attend because I was recovering from illness, one of the Scriptures that was apparently prominent was Ezekiel 37. Although I was not there at the meeting, a number of people (I am told) felt very strongly that this passage was not just something that I personally needed to read, but it was also a word to our house church network. So, I spent some time in this passage, felt God say some things to me about it, and then felt urged to pass on to you the contents of this letter.

I believe that Ezekiel 37 is speaking to us as a cluster of churches about either a step-by-step process, or parallel process, that the Lord wants and needs to take us through to fulfill the plans he has for us. There are 6 stages to this process.

Firstly, Ezekiel 37:7-8 speaks of organization and structure. This passage is about bones and skin and tendons and ligaments and joints all coming together properly to create a body. There is a pattern, a form, an organizational scheme, a blueprint that we are to have as a house church network. Not man-made, pragmatic, synthetic structures that many of the institutional churches of past and present are using. But, rather, the apostolic New Testament way of organizing churches. This means things like using homes and house-sized groups, grassroots unpaid local leadership, open and participatory meetings, occasional traveling apostles and teachers, the self-governing nature of each house church, etc. Okay, now we have a properly designed "car body", but now we need fuel to make it run; thus the next point.

Secondly, Ezekiel 37:9-10 speaks of life and energy. This passage talks about breathing life and air into the body so that it can start moving around. Obviously, without gas, a car is useless. Similarly, we need the Spirit of God to breathe himself into us as individuals and into our house church structures. Otherwise, it's all pointless. What needs to happen for us to recapture and grow in our passion for Christ? What about our passion for those in darkness without God and hope in the world? What do we need to repent of and change? What do we need to experience from God to be set aflame again?

Thirdly, Ezekiel 37:16-22 speaks of unity and teamwork as the next stage or factor. This passage speaks of God joining two sticks together into one stick so that they will be one in his hand—one single spiritual baseball bat that God can use to hit that grand slam out of the ballpark. I believe God is wanting to unite us in purpose and passion as a house church network and to work together closely to accomplish his plans. I don't mean organizational unity under some leadership pyramid scheme, but rather unity of heart and mind and direction. But for this to happen, there needs to be unity and teamwork in our individual house churches. Are there tensions that need to be resolved? Is there repentance and forgiveness that needs to happen? Is somebody slacking or hiding or not really being honest with the group? This is something to pray and act on.

Fourthly, Ezekiel 37:23-24 speaks of holiness and obedience. This passage talks about getting rid of idols and detestable things and transgressions and cleansing. God says he will deliver and cleanse us, and then we will be his people and keep his commands. This is tough stuff. We all know ourselves well enough to see most of our flaws and little obsessions and idols and other hidden agendas and schemes. God knows we're but dust. Yet, he loves us and likes us anyway, but we do have a responsibility and desperate need to get rid of the crap in our lives. Are we ready, willing, and able?

Fifthly, Ezekiel 37:26 speaks of growth and multiplication of God's people. Yes, numerical growth folks! I do not believe for one second that a healthy and vibrant network of house churches is something God wants to keep small and forever hidden. Quantity comes from quality. But, this is all in God's timing and schedule, not ours. He will lead us to branch out and call people to start new house churches, to bring new people into existing groups, and to multiply current groups into two. This is a Spirit-led process. I am convinced it will come in due time. All we need to do is be faithful to what God is asking of us in this moment and walk through the doors he swings wide open for us. This is a tough thing. So be it! It's not about our agendas anyway.

Sixthly, Ezekiel 37:28 speaks of a broader influence on the nations. Do we really, honestly, truly believe that God can and wants to use you and me to touch the city we live in, our region, our country, and even the nations? How exactly this happens is another matter. It may mean touching one person's life somewhere else on this crazy planet, or it may mean many. God knows. Remember Abraham—long beard, a little older than we are, no kids? Well, God promised him that the nations of the world would be impacted by his life because he believed God—not just that he believed in God—but, rather, that he believed what God had promised. Well, you all know how that turned out through the eventual birth of Jesus Christ through the long line of Abraham's descendants. Bang!!! History changed forever! You and I are also part of this plan too to bless the world. Dare we step ahead to see God's promises to us fulfilled through us?

So, there it is. Pray about it if you want. Think about it. May we obey what the Spirit says to us individually and as a team of house churches.

With much affection in Christ,
Rad Zdero

Letter #2
The following is a letter I sent to another fledgling network of house churches that was about to embark on cohesive partnership together in their region. I had no hand in starting this network, other than encouraging the main catalyzer to be bold and step forward to link the groups. My personal relationship over the years with the key catalyzer of this cluster of groups gave me a platform to communicate the following to the team he was facilitating. The letter was read at one of the first gatherings of the leaders of this network.

Dear Sisters and Brothers,
Those of us here in our region of the country, who share a common faith and mission with you, greet you heartily!

We are convinced that God, at this time in history, is once again drawing out a remnant of believers who will accomplish his kingdom agenda.

Therefore, as you gather together today to dream and scheme with God and to stand in the gap for your region of our fair nation, we want to cheer you on. Be assured that we stand with you as you embark on discovering what linking your house churches together will look like. It will be a challenge, but it will also be an adventure.

May this be the first of many Spirit-led and Scripture-based steps in working together to make an impact for Christ on the families, factories, offices, shops, schools, neighbourhoods, and towns in your part of the nation.

In our region of the country, we have come from a long way off and a long way down to get to the point of trusting each other enough to partner together in linking our simple, organic, house churches into a functional body. But, we have desired and determined to do this without the trappings of institutionalism. We have, therefore, purposed to network together our house churches in a way that is relational (rather than organizational), intentional (rather than accidental), and missional (rather than aimless).

We have found such networking not only to be biblical (Acts 2:41-47, 20:20), but also strategic and practical. We have been able to accomplish far more together in our region as a cluster of house churches, rather than apart as isolated house churches. May we encourage you, as you step forward in this, to be truly open to the potential of partnering with each other. This will require trust, sacrifice, commitment, and passion on your part.

And so, if there is anything we can do, please let us know. We trust that we also have much to gain from your experiences, knowledge, giftings, and resources. Full steam ahead! Don't look back!

On behalf of the company of the faithful here,
Rad Zdero

Letter #3

The following letter is a typical one sent to a loose network of about 20 to 25 house church leaders to participate in one of the several "think tank" gatherings we had in my region. This included people who were apostles, prophets, elders, and prayer intercessors. The purpose was to get to know each other better so that personal trust, practical partnership, and cross-pollination could begin.

Hello Friends,

Expecting all is well with you. A few of us have been in touch and feel the time has come for another regional house church leaders meeting. It is "think tank" time again!

Why? I am very excited personally about the ways God has been bringing us together gently in this region into unity relationally, by cross-pollination, and as various ones of us have actually co-laboured together in different contexts. Only recently have I felt really free to speak openly about some things God revealed in a dream to me over a year ago, after several confirmations. The long and short of it is this: "God is not satisfied with denominations, but is drawing out a remnant for himself that will accomplish his will." And that we must "prepare for revival" in our region. Are we ready? This does not mean organizational unity. But, rather, this means setting into place some tangible expressions of relational, intentional, and missional unity, and moving from simply being aware of one another's existence to actually partnering together over the long haul. The whole is greater than the sum of the parts. We cannot do this alone in our own "backyards."

What? We will spend part of the day together updating, reconnecting, praying, and worshipping. Then we will transition into processing through an article entitled "The power of partnerships." There are also a few decisions/discussions that should be made about this year's conference, the possibility of a common regional apostolic fund that we can donate to voluntarily as God leads, and how to best use the *Starfish Files* house church magazine. Hard copies of the latest issue will be available for each of us. Details of invitees, location, date, and time are attached.

Please let me know if you are able to attend as soon as possible. If you cannot come, would you consider having one of your key people attend?

Viva la revolucion!
Rad Zdero

Letter #4

The following letter was sent to a loose network of house church leaders, who were the same people as in Letter #3 above. Its aim was as a follow-up to a "think tank" meeting of these leaders who spent a day together just building relationships and exploring the idea of partnership. It took several of these gatherings over a period of several years to develop trust.

Hello Friends!

Just a quick note to follow-up on the regional house church meeting this past Saturday. First, please find attached in Microsoft Word below a contact list for attendees and invitees who were not able to make it out. Second, see the notes from our small group and large group time about ideas regarding partnerships and networking. What we want and what we do not want. Third, set aside the date indicated for the first regional house church movement weekend retreat. The retreat centre is already booked. There is room for about 50 overnighters, but more for day visitors. This is a cozy, spacious, heated facility suitable for kids of all ages, with 2 kitchens, 2 living rooms, a large central gathering place, and numerous bedrooms. Cost and other details will be emailed out as the time approaches. On a personal note, I was immensely encouraged by our time together. There is so much potential in each of us individually and as we partner together to be some small part of seeing God's empire break out all across the region!

Thanks for your friendship,
Rad Zdero

Letter #5

The following letter was sent to a very scattered group of house church leaders and several traditional pastors I knew to inform them of a multi-city speaking and visiting tour I was planning across our region. The tour did not happen until 2 years after this initial letter was sent. It involved driving 2200 kilometers to visit leaders and groups in 7 cities over a period of 2 weeks in one continuous circuit. It was a success in many ways and a learning experience for me, but it was very tiring.

Hello Friends!

I hope you are all prospering in body and spirit. Personally, I am doing very well, and the Lord has really been keeping his eye on me in many ways. Allow me to inform you of an opportunity for you to prayerfully consider.

What? I am currently planning a speaking tour to visit the emerging house churches in the region. During these visits, I will be giving a seminar-style teaching on the history of the house church movement. We will explore 2000 years of church history with practical implications for us today on the North American house church scene. Copies of my book *The Global House Church Movement*, which some of you have read, will be available for purchase. Also, a small team of 2 to 3 friends with musical and prophetic gifts may come along to minister to your group as the Lord leads.

Why? Firstly, through some prophetic words from trusted friends as well as personal prayer and reflection, I believe the Lord is asking us to offer this service to the wider body of Christ. Secondly, this seminar could supplement your current training of cell group and/or house church leaders and may be a good introduction to those in your circle who are just asking questions.

Where? The tour will involve towns and cities across our region.

When? If you are interested in hosting this seminar for your house church or house church leaders, please feel free to contact me to discuss details and dates.

What this is not! Finally, please note that I will not be accepting any money for my personal benefit. Any money from the purchase of the books and freewill donations will go directly into the ministry fund of the house church network in which I participate.

Friends, thanks again for your consideration. May the peace of Christ go with you,

Rad Zdero

Letter #6
This short note was written in response to a series of email exchanges between house church leaders in preparation for a national network meeting for key leaders which I was organizing. A few emails between some people were becoming tense. A friend encouraged me—since I was the facilitator of the email exchange and the upcoming meeting—to write a note to calm things down. It is always a challenge to see a solid network emerge among leaders who are passionate about their own ideas.

Hello Ladies and Gentlemen,

I have read with great interest the various emails back and forth. I appreciate the variety of ideas, warnings, and encouragements. It is this kind of cross-pollination that we each need, because each of us has unique blind spots, baggage, emphases, weaknesses, strengths, perspectives, experiences, and gifts. It is clear that passion is in the air for the Lord and his work. I would simply add this. Let us learn from one another, not presuming we have all the answers. Let the conversation be encouraging, not critical of each other. Let us talk to each other, not shout over each other. Let us take time to think and pray, before we immediately respond to each other. Let us treat each other as Christ would. We are all in this together, if we choose to be.

Rad Zdero

11

LETTER TO A NATIONWIDE HOUSE CHURCH MOVEMENT

This letter was sent to a nationwide movement of house churches in an Asian nation. One of their key apostolic leaders, with whom I had regular contact, invited me to write a letter of encouragement to their network as they stepped forward in carrying out exploits for God's empire in their country.

Dear Friends,

Some time back you invited me to write a letter of encouragement to your nationwide network—in fact, your thriving movement—of house churches. I feel humbled and grateful for the chance to do so. Of course, modesty prevents me from being too enthusiastic about the idea because I feel I too am always learning and growing in this thing that God is presently doing on the earth by restoring his grassroots church. But, equally, false modesty might prevent me from writing anything at all and miss the opportunity for me to share what I have from the Lord for you and for us to connect on a deeper level with one another. And so I have taken your invitation soberly. What I would like to do is simply highlight some important elements that I believe any Spirit-led,

Scripture-based, and strategy-driven network of simple, organic, house churches should endeavour to include in their midst. I want to first remind us of what God has done in history, and is doing today, through small group and house church movements and then move on to give 10 specific points for your national network to consider.

The God of History

God has often shaped the last 2000 years of history through church planting movements (CPMs), mainly in the form of simple, grassroots, small groups and house churches. A CPM is a rapid multiplication of churches planting churches over a sustained period of time. A CPM is not just another man-made tactic or trend. It is, in fact, God's work. And its purpose is to see people come to a saving encounter with Jesus Christ, grow in spiritual maturity, and then become change agents for God.

The first CPM, of course, is recorded in the New Testament, where we read about the Holy Spirit prompting the early followers of Christ to start a multiplying movement of simple churches. Christ sent believers into the world to make disciples, baptize converts, and teach them to follow him fully (Matt 28:18-20; Acts 1:8). Apostles sowed the gospel in new geographic, cultural, and linguistic soil and felt an urgency to begin disciplemaking communities across the Roman world (Acts 13:1-3; 1 Cor 9:16-17; 1 Tim 2:7). Elders were more mature believers who nurtured a local body of believers and gave direction at certain decision-making times (Acts 15:2-6,22; 1 Tim 4:14,5:17; Titus 1:5-11; Heb 13:7,17). These churches met primarily in homes, but also in large group contexts for training, healing, and evangelism (Acts 2:46, 5:12, 5:42, 8:5-8, 10:1-48, 16:15, 20:20; Rom 16:3-5; 1 Cor 16:19; Col 4:15; Philem 1:2). Church meetings were Spirit-led, interactive, and participatory as all believers used their gifts and abilities (1 Cor 14:26; Eph 5:19-20; Col 3:16; Heb 10:25). And these house churches were connected together into an outwardly expanding network at citywide, regional, and empire-wide levels (Acts 2:41-47, 5:12, 5:42, 15:3,36,41, 20:20; Gal 2:9-10). They turned the world upside down (Acts 17:6).

The following centuries were filled with stories of CPMs as people let go (to one degree or another) of the trappings of religious institutions to grab hold of a living breathing Christianity. Pachomius (290-346 AD) began a network of home-based monastic groups of a dozen members in response to the flaws of the institutional church. Priscillian (340-385 AD) and his followers multiplied home-based "brotherhoods" across Spain, France, and Portugal before being wiped out by the institutional church. Patrick (390-460 AD) started a missionary movement in Ireland that sent teams to take the gospel throughout the nations of northwestern Europe. Peter Waldo (1150-1206 AD) and his Waldenses drew a third of western Christendom to their public and home gatherings. The Anabaptists (c.1520) of central Europe, who often met in secret home groups, grew to tens of thousands over a period of 80 years. The Quakers (c.1650) in Britain recruited 20,000 new members in a few years. The Moravians (c.1750) sent 3,000 missionaries to many parts of the globe. The Methodists (c.1750) in Britain and America by 1791 grew to 10,000 home groups and ignited the First Great Awakening. They saw many thousands of people changed and reconciled back to God in their generation. And they served as an example to others who would follow, not only about the victories that were possible by going back to the blueprint of the New Testament church, but also about the persecutions, criticisms, betrayals, and other difficulties that should be expected.

Today, CPMs are also everywhere. In China, the church has grown from 1 to 2 million believers in 1949 to almost 100 million believers today in underground house churches. In India, about 1 million house churches have been started between 1995 and 2009. In the USA, Church Multiplication Associates recently planted 1000 simple churches in 7 short years at home and abroad. In Ethiopia, the Meserete Kristos Church, which is a Pentecostal denomination, grew rapidly in the 1980s from 5000 to 50,000 members only after they went into underground house groups to avoid persecution by the Marxist regime. In Latin America, the Basic Christian Communities, which are house church-type groups, started in the 1960s among the marginalized and have grown to 1 million groups by 2007.

Past and present CPMs have been analyzed with modern research tools to discover key elements for high-quality rapid church growth. CPMs have been well-documented in E.H. Broadbent's *The Pilgrim Church* (1931), John Driver's *Radical Faith: An Alternative History of the Christian Church* (1999), Peter Bunton's *Cell Groups and House Churches: What History Teaches Us* (2001), David Garrison's *Church Planting Movements* (2004), and my own books *The Global House Church Movement* (2004) and *Nexus: The World House Church Movement Reader* (2007). I would recommend getting your hands on one or several of these resources and use them to inspire and instruct the house churches with whom you are in contact, so that they will be better equipped with practical tools, intellectual insights, and moving stories to impact your entire nation with a saturation church planting movement.

Let me now briefly remind you about some of the vital elements often mentioned by students of CPMs. Perhaps more importantly, I wish to point out other factors that are almost never discussed. But, none of what I am about to write should be implemented mechanically in a contrived fashion, as if assembling these puzzle pieces will bring about God's presence and a great harvest of souls. I am not trying to promote any kind of formula to see a CPM emerge. Instead, as you look to God and run after his wisdom, I believe the Lord wants to give you strategies about how and when to implement the following elements. With that acknowledged, let us now recognize that everything in the world has an anatomy, a geometry, a shape—and so do CPMs. And so, with that said, let us now briefly highlight some specifics.

The Big Picture

Some house churches wander about aimlessly. They have no direction and make no real impact. Some realize this is a problem, while others wrongly take pride in this and even mistake it for being "Spirit-led." But, there is a better way! House churches that wish to thrive, grow, multiply, and make a difference must be captivated by a bigger vision beyond themselves.

The Bible tells us that "where there is no vision, the people perish" (Prov 29:18, KJV) and "except the Lord build the house, they labor in vain that build it" (Psalm 127:1, KJV). Certainly, the early church was often directed supernaturally and spontaneously in the moment before taking any action (Acts 8:26-40, 10:1-48, 13:1-4). But, it was the Great Commission mission statement of Jesus that gave the apostles and the rest of the church a clear mandate for all they did (Matt 28:18-20; Mark 16:15-16; Luke 24:46-49; John 20:21-23; Acts 1:8).

Your house churches today, therefore, must get hold of what God is saying to them before they launch out. You must get the big picture of God's main purpose for you locally, regionally, and nationally. I urge you to pray, fast, receive God's supernatural power, watch the circumstances, discern your contexts, talk together, set measurable goals, and even craft mission statements. This can start in each house church, but must also happen among leadership teams of elders and apostles across your country.

The Right D.N.A.

Some house churches are unbalanced. They are strong in some things and weak in others. Instead of seeking to grow in their areas of weakness, they continue to operate only in their strengths. This is certainly a recipe for going nowhere fast. But, there is a better way! House churches that wish to be vibrant must have the right D.N.A., as noted by Neil Cole of Church Multiplication Associates.

D refers to Divine Truth and should include Bible study and allow for prophetic words, dreams, visions, miracles, and godly counsel. *N* stands for Nurturing Relationships and should involve honesty, affection, and practically doing life together. *A* means Apostolic Mission and should include reaching out in word and deed to family, friends, neighbours, workmates, and strangers. The early church had a good measure of the *D*, the *N*, and the *A* (Acts 2:41-47).

Your house churches today, therefore, must be brutally honest with themselves and take stock of whether they have the right D.N.A. for God to work through them. The D.N.A. should not be unraveled, but should be fully present within each individual believer, each house church, each leadership team of elders and/or apostles, and each network of house churches on local, regional, and national levels.

An Army of Leaders

Some house churches reject the whole issue of leadership because they feel that Christ alone is the only leader of their group or because they have been hurt by institutional leaders in the past. Some believe that only professional, seminary-trained, and denominationally-ordained clergy persons are legitimate leaders that can give proper spiritual covering to their house church. Some assert, on the other extreme, that every believer is, in fact, a leader in the real sense. But, there is a better way! House churches must look to the Scriptures and the Spirit to allow for the emergence of God-given leaders in their midst.

These extremes among some house churches of rejecting any kind of leadership, assuming that all believers are leaders, or looking only to ordained institutional clergy must be rejected altogether precisely because none of these are biblical ideas. Rather, we see in the New Testament that all believers were encouraged to use their abilities and gifts for the benefit of others in the Body of Christ (1 Pet 2:5-9; 1 Cor 12:1-31, 14:1-40). But, they also recognized two main types of leaders, namely, local elders (Acts 14:23, 1 Tim 3:1-7; Tit 1:5-9; 1 Pet 5:1-5) and translocal apostles (Act 13:1-4, 15:6; Eph 4:11) to equip the church and reach the world.

Your house churches today, therefore, must also encourage the emergence of healthy leaders. *Micro leaders* (or elders) are unpaid spiritual moms and dads who nurture, train, and empower believers in their house church to do the work of the ministry. *Macro leaders* (or apostles) are pioneers, visionaries, and strategists who start new house churches, adopt existing house churches, link them together into networks, and then move on to repeat the process, and who should be financially supported when needed and when possible. I urge you to be vigilant to discern the leaders that are emerging from your house churches, give them opportunities to connect with each other, train them thoroughly in understanding the Bible, and give them practical instruction on how to effectively carry out their tasks.

Networking Your Groups and Leaders

Some house churches are utterly isolated due to circumstances. They soon become ingrown and irrelevant and eventually implode. Isolated groups simply do not work. Others create formal organizations that "brand" their house churches just like denominations with their various branch churches. And they will not work closely with others because they are of a different "brand". Even worse, some house churches refuse to work with other house churches in the same town because of competition, limited vision, or petty differences. But, there is a better way! House churches that want to be fruitful must link arms with others nearby, relationally but cohesively.

The early house churches partnered together as citywide networks in Jerusalem (Acts 2:41-47), Rome (Rom 16:3-15), and Ephesus (Acts 20:17,20), and as a regional network in Asia Minor (2 and 3 John; Rev 2 and 3). They were linked through leaders meetings (Acts 15:6, 20:17), large group events (Acts 2:44, 5:12, 20:20), apostolic visits (Acts 14:23, 15:36; 3 John 1:5-8), and apostolic letters (Acts 15:22-23).

Your house churches today, therefore, must form relational, but cohesive, networks with others nearby in the cities and regions of your nation. Those who wish to continue labouring in isolation should be left to follow their own path, after several encouragements to plug into a network. Such partnership cannot be forced on anyone. But as for you, face-to-face cross-pollination will allow you to pool your resources, share experiences, permit accountability, engage in training, meet your own social needs, and impact an entire city or region. You will be able to accomplish far more together than you can separately.

Money and Resources

Some house churches have abandoned giving money or resources to mission at all. Because they rightly believe that 10% tithing is not a New Testament practice, they wrongly conclude they do not need to give at all. And they have become stingy and selfish with the things God has given them. Consequently, many things God wants accomplished never get done through these folks. But, there is a better way! House churches that wish to make a difference must take the locks off their wallets, open up their hearts and hands, and begin to give generously to God's mission.

The early Christians were taught to give gladly. There were two groups of people they mainly gave money and resources to, namely, those in dire need (Acts 2:44-45, 4:32-35; 1 Cor 16:1-3; 2 Cor 9:1-15) and apostolic workers (Luke 10:7-8; 1 Cor 9:1-18; Philip 4:10-20).

Your house churches today, therefore, must ask God where he wants them to give. Each house church or network can do several practical things. They can give money to their own bank account or money bag. They can circulate amongst themselves good teaching resources such as books and videos. They can help the poor and destitute locally and abroad. They can give finances to apostles and apostolic projects that help house churches learn, grow, and connect with one another.

Cultural Context

Some house churches are completely uninterested in (or unaware of) the economic, religious, philosophical, linguistic, political, artistic, and technological factors that shape their culture. So, their attempts at impacting non-believers and reaching church drop-outs are ineffective. But, there is a better way! House churches that want to influence people must be students of, and participants in, mainstream culture except, of course, without sinning.

The early Christians related the good news of Jesus using culturally relevant methods (1 Cor 9:19-23). To fellow Jews, Peter would retell the familiar story of God's dealings with the people of Israel and how Jesus was the fulfillment of that drama (Acts

2:14-41, 3:11-26). To philosophical Athenians, Paul felt free to quote from pagan religious inscriptions and poets to make his argument (Acts 17:16-34). Jesus, too, told simple stories about daily life to ordinary people (Matt 13:1-52), while debating theology with religious leaders (Mark 12:13-40).

Your house churches today, therefore, must engage society in relevant ways and live lifestyles that others can relate to. Have you seen the latest popular movie? Did you read the best-selling book in your country? Do you know about the economic issues shaping your city, region, or nation? Have you studied the world's religions and cults, especially those that are prevalent in your country? If so, you will be much more effective in engaging people in spiritual conversations.

The Lord of Time

Some house church people want to grow and multiply easily and quickly. This is an understandable and noble desire. But, when they discover that God often takes a long time to do things, they quit. These folks are not true world-changers. Maybe they are not actually called by God to the work. Maybe they are fickle pragmatists with little real conviction. Maybe they are immature believers. But, there is a better way! House churches must recognize that our God is the Lord of Time who often takes longer to put his plans into action than we sometimes want.

Abraham waited 25 years before God fulfilled his promise of giving him a son. Moses spent 40 years in exile tending sheep before God called him to free Israel from Egyptian bondage. Joseph went through 20 years of obscurity, betrayal, imprisonment, and suffering before he became Pharaoh's second-in-command over the entire nation of Egypt and in a position to rescue his family—the seed of Abraham—from the ravages of famine, thus fulfilling the vision that God gave him when he was a young lad of 17 years. David waited 17 years after his anointing by the prophet Samuel before becoming king. Jesus spent 30 years in obscurity before launching his public ministry. Paul had to wait about 10 years after his conversion before actually being sent from Antioch as an apostle to the Gentiles.

Your house churches today, therefore, must be in this for the long haul if you are to see God firmly establish his "household strategy" among your neighbourhoods, villages, towns, cities, regions, and nation. I urge you to wait on God, watch the circumstances, and discern the times and seasons that God has appointed for the house church movement in your nation.

Blood, Sweat, and Tears

Some house church people are absolutely unprepared to endure the necessary hardships and do what it takes to see God accomplish his purposes through them. They will only be involved if personal sacrifice is not required. But, there is a better way! House churches that want to produce quality disciples of Christ must be ready to be refined by the fire.

Jesus and his early followers knew this well. They spilt their blood as they were physically persecuted by civil authorities, religious leaders, and lynch mobs through arrests, trials, imprisonments, beatings, stonings, and assassination attempts (John 19:1-30; Acts 4:1-7, 5:17-27, 7:54-60, 8:1-3, 19:23-41, 23:12-22; 2 Cor 11:23-25). They poured their sweat from the hard work of praying, evangelizing, healing, teaching, traveling, battling physical hardship, and persisting in their concern for the churches (Mark 3:20; Luke 6:12, 8:1, 9:6; Acts 1:14; 2 Cor 11:23,26-28). They shed their tears as they were denied, betrayed, abandoned, and criticized by family, friends, and fellow Christians (Matt 10:34-37; Mark 3:21, 6:1-4; John 6:66, 18:1-3, 18:25-27; 2 Cor 10:10; Philip 1:15-17; 2 Tim 4:10,16).

Your house churches today, therefore, must be ready to expend blood, sweat, and tears, for God is asking you to help repair the broken foundations of his church in order to reach your nation.

Laser Beam Focus

Some house church people are not fully engaged and are not fully committed to God's agenda. They are dabblers. They are sometimes too distracted by hobbies, ambitions, sinful habits, and participation in some good institutional church ministries. But, there is a better way! We must fully dedicate our time, energy, abilities, passions, and resources into the local, regional, and global house church movement that God is raising up today.

Anyone who puts other relationships ahead of following Jesus cannot be his disciple (Luke 14:26). Anyone who puts their hand to the plow and keeps looking back is not fit for the kingdom (Luke 9:62). Anyone who does not count the cost before embarking on a new venture will often fail (Luke 14:28-30). Anyone who allows the worries, riches, and pleasures of this life to dominate them will never bear fruit (Luke 8:14). Anyone who perpetually practices sin will get entangled and enslaved (John 8:34-36; Heb 12:1-2; 1 John 1:6-10, 5:18).

Your house churches today, therefore, must focus like a laser beam on the specific task God has for them. You must never allow the good things in life to replace the God things in life. You must sweep aside anything that would slow you down. You must run the race to win.

Personal Calling

Some house church believers have not been genuinely called by the Spirit to get involved in this new, yet ancient, way of being the church. Maybe they are just looking for quick church growth results. Maybe they just want to follow the latest Christian trend. Maybe they just want a platform for their personal ministry. Maybe they are just reacting to past emotional hurts from institutional churches. Maybe they are just looking for a comfortable fellowship to belong to. But, there is a better way! House churches should gently encourage their members to do some real soul searching before God to figure out if they really should be involved at all.

Noah was called to help save a remnant from the flood of judgment (Gen 6:13-22). Moses was called to help deliver the Hebrews from Egyptian slavery (Exod 3:10). Gideon was called to deliver God's people from the Midianites (Judges 6:14). Jesus was called to rescue the world from the spiritual darkness of sin by his sacrificial death on the cross (John 3:16). Paul was called to be the chief apostle to the Gentiles (Acts 9:15-17, 13:1-3). And only because they were genuinely invited by the Spirit to put their hand to the task did they fulfill their mission.

Your house churches today, therefore, must be 100% sure that the Spirit has truly summoned them personally to do what they are doing. If you are unsure at all, you may indeed be messing things up. So, you had better get into your proverbial prayer closets and stay there until you get an answer one way or another. Only then will you be able to endure the trials and accomplish the tasks that lay ahead.

Thanks again for the privilege of writing this letter to your national network of house churches. My hope is that God will use this meager offering and magnify it to help spiritually feed your emerging house churches, in the same way Jesus greatly multiplied the humble offering of a few fish and some bread brought to him. If I may be bold, may I say that I believe you must seriously consider and prayerfully implement these factors, among other things, to see God's grand purposes accomplished in your country through the simple, organic, house church movement today. May Jesus Christ continue to get his spotless Bride ready in your nation and allow you to have victory in his holy revolutionary struggle!

All good things to you,
Rad Zdero

SUBJECT INDEX

A
accountability, 19,23,27,28,31,81, 86,119,136,154
Anabaptist(s), 24,84,150
apostle(s), 92,98,114,117, 121,122,128-138,153

B
baptize(d), 19,89,149
bishop(s), 51,92,101,121

C
Calvin, John, 131
Catholic, 63-65,68,71,73-75
cell church(es), 18,67,70,74, 88,89,94,103
cell group(s), 18,68,70,74, 76,87,108,119,146,151
children, 23,55,59,120,121, 123
China, xi,64,65,84,86,89,105, 121,150
church building(s), 26,79,88,90
church plant(er)(ing), 86,104, 106,107,110,111,133,149,151
circuit rider(s), 19,43,125
citywide, 19,31,82,85,86,88, 136,149,154
clergy, 65,67,117,153
Communist(s), 64

community, 17,22,27,32,39,64, 79,80,88,130,137
Constantine, 79
culture(s), 52,62,63,134,155

D
denomination(al)(s), 49,66-71, 96-111, 129,144,150,153,154
disciple(s)(ship), 17,18,58, 65,80,86, 114,133,134, 157,158
doctrine(s), 29,30,33,51,72, 107,129

E
early church father(s), 121
ekklesia, 80-82
elder(s), 19,51,70,92,100,101, 113-119,123,138,152,153
evangelism, 43,69,75,82,86, 137,149
evangelist(ic)(s), xi,26,43,51,65, 83,87,89,102,137,138

F
finance(d)(s), 20,65,90-92, 100-102, 109,124,135,155
Fox, George, 131
Francis of Assisi, 65

161

G
Great Commission, 152

I
institutional church, xi,26,63, 70,74, 90-92,126,157,158

L
leader(s)(ship), 49-51, 100-102,113, 114,116, 132-137,153,154
Lord's Supper, 19,76,81,84
Luther, Martin, 68,131

M
Methodist(s), 24,136,150
money, 28,29,57,90-92,101, 106,135,138,147,155
Moravian(s), 150
Mystery Babylon, 62-65,67, 68,70,71,73-75

N
network(ing)(s), 17-21,30,31,43, 82,88,101-105,118,119, 140-145,154

O
oikos, 52,80
overseer(s), 51,92,101,123

P
participatory, 27,84,108,140,149
pastor(s), 26,42,45,51,55,90, 92,101,103,106-108,123, 129,138
Patrick of Ireland, 24,150
Pentecostal(s), 24,66,150
persecution, 105,134,137,150
presbyter(s), 92,101
Priscillian(ists), 24,150

prophet(s), 42-44,51,54,67, 120,131-132,137,138

Q
Quakers, 24,84,150

R
revival, 18,131,144

S
shepherd(s), 28,92,101,123
signs, 30,35
spiritual gift(s), 18,33,41,46, 52,54,55

T
teacher(s), 51,53,70,129, 137,138,140
temple(s), 26,89,98
tithing, 92,96-102
tradition(al)(s), 46,62-65,69,84,85
train(ing), 19,26,31,32,59, 103,114,117-119,133-135

W
Waldo, Peter, 150
Waldenses, 24,150
Wesley, John, 65,68,69,71, 74,131,135-137
women, 48-60,121-123
Wycliffe, John, 131

Z
Zinzendorf, 68
Zwingli, 68

ABOUT THE AUTHOR

R AD ZDERO has a Ph.D. degree in Mechanical Engineering, with a specialty in bio-mechanics and bio-materials. He is the director of a hospital-based research team. He enjoys long walks, epic movies, books, poetry, short stories, music, coffee shops, and peaceful revolutions. Rad has been actively involved in the house church and small group movement since 1985. He is dedicated to the emergence of the worldwide house church phenomenon and seeing the power and pattern of New Testament Christianity fully restored in our day. He is the author of *The Global House Church Movement* (2004) and the editor of *Nexus: The World House Church Movement Reader* (2007). His novel *Entopia: Revolution of the Ants* (2008) is an allegorical tale of grassroots revolution inside the hierarchical and ordered world of an anthill. And he is also the editor of *The Starfish Files* house church magazine, which has an international readership. Inquiries about potential translation projects of this book, *Letters to the House Church Movement*, should be sent to the author:

ADDRESS
Rad Zdero
P.O. Box 39528
Lakeshore P.O.
Mississauga, ON
Canada L5G-4S6

W: www.scribd.com/rzdero
E: rzdero@yahoo.ca

More Books by RAD ZDERO

THE GLOBAL HOUSE CHURCH MOVEMENT

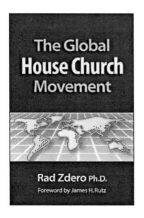

Biblical, historical, and practical insights to help you start a house church network no matter where you live! Guaranteed to challenge your understanding of what the church is really all about!

A primer that's perfect for ...
- House churches and small groups
- Christian leaders of all types
- Church planters and missionaries

... and others who believe that small groups are the best way to reach people and disciple them in Christ !

~ Paperback ~ 155 pages ~

To Order at Best Price:
Tel: 1-800-647-7466 (Inside USA)
Tel: 1-706-554-1594 (Outside USA)
Secure Online Ordering at
www.MissionBooks.org

More Books by RAD ZDERO

NEXUS: THE WORLD HOUSE CHURCH MOVEMENT READER

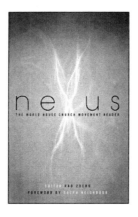

Welcome to the Nexus, your point of connection to the world house church movement! Grassroots Christianity is exploding around the world through saturation church planting of simple, inexpensive, participatory, reproducible, autonomous, and missional house churches. As the editor, Rad Zdero has compiled the writings of almost 40 leaders, practitioners, and scholars from around the world. The authors have contributed their insight and experience in over 60 provocative articles, which inform, inspire, and invite you to start your own network of multiplying house churches no matter where you live.

~ Paperback ~ 528 pages ~

To Order at Best Price:
Tel: 1-800-647-7466 (Inside USA)
Tel: 1-706-554-1594 (Outside USA)
Secure online ordering from
www.MissionBooks.org

More Books by RAD ZDERO

ENTOPIA: REVOLUTION OF THE ANTS

In the allegorical tradition of George Orwell's Animal Farm.

It is a world of hierarchy and order. And Gazer is but an ordinary worker ant living in the ancient ant colony of Entgora. After a mishap during a routine work expedition sends her plummeting to the ground, snapping off one of her antennae, Gazer stumbles across the sacred but secret mating ritual of a future Queen ant. The night before her trial for this blasphemy and crime, she has a dream that changes the course of her life and the lives of all antkind from that day on. Along with her friends Tenspeed and Digdirt, Gazer finds herself locked in a whirlwind of political and mystical intrigues, epic ant wars and civil revolts, gender and class struggles, dreams and secret societies, all culminating in a bittersweet end.

~ Paperback ~ 132 pages ~

To Order
*Tel: 1-540-882-9062, Fax: 1-540-882-3719
Secure Online Ordering at
www.oaktara.com and www.amazon.com*

CPSIA information can be obtained at www.ICGtesting.com
Printed in the USA
BVOW050557140911

271223BV00001B/149/P